TEN
WINDOWS

TEN
WINDOWS

How Great Poems Transform the World

JANE
HIRSHFIELD

Alfred A. Knopf, New York 2015

Library of Congress Cataloging-in-Publication Data

Hirshfield, Jane, 1953–

[Essays. Selections]

Ten windows : how great poems transform the world / Jane Hirshfield.—First edition.

pages ; cm

"This is a Borzoi book."

ISBN 978-0-385-35105-8 (hardcover) — ISBN 978-0-385-35106-5 (eBook)

I. Title.

PS3558.I694A6 2015

814'.54—dc23   2014025430

Jacket image: St. Augustine in His Study (detail) by Vittore Carpaccio.
S. Giorgio degli Schiavoni, Venice, Italy. Scala / Art Resource, N.Y.
Jacket design by Carol Devine Carson

Manufactured in the United States of America
Published March 18, 2015
Reprinted One Time
Third Printing, May 2015

CONTENTS

PREFACE

Good art is a truing of vision, in the way a saw is trued in the saw shop, to cut more cleanly. It is also a changing of vision. Entering a good poem, a person feels, tastes, hears, thinks, and sees in altered ways. Why ask art into a life at all, if not to be transformed and enlarged by its presence and mysterious means? Some hunger for *more* is in us—more range, more depth, more feeling; more associative freedom, more beauty. More perplexity and more friction of interest. More prismatic grief and unstunted delight, more longing, more darkness. More saturation and permeability in knowing our own existence as also the existence of others. More capacity to be astonished. Art adds to the sum of the lives we would have, were it possible to live without it. And by changing selves, one by one, art changes also the outer world that selves create and share.

This book continues the investigation begun in an earlier volume, *Nine Gates: Entering the Mind of Poetry.* The questions pursued by poems themselves are speckled, partial, and infinite. These books, though, pursue as well a single question: How do poems—how does art—work? Under that question, inevitably, is another: How do we? Inside the intricate clockworks of language and music, event and life, what allows and invites us to feel and know as we do, and then increase our feeling and knowing? Such a question cannot be answered. "We" are different, from one another and, moment by moment, from even ourselves. "Art," too, is a word deceptively single of surface. Still, following this question for thirty years has given me pleasure, and some sense of approaching more nearly a destination whose center cannot ever be mapped or reached.

TEN
WINDOWS

CHAPTER ONE

Kingfishers Catching Fire:
Looking with Poetry's Eyes

A mysterious quickening inhabits the depths of any good poem—protean, elusive, alive in its own right. The word "creative" shares its etymology with the word "creature," and carries a similar sense of breathing aliveness, of an active, fine-grained, and multicellular making. What is creative is rooted in growth and rising, in the bringing into existence of new and autonomous being. We feel something stir, shiver, swim its way into the world when a good poem opens its eyes. Poetry's work is not simply the recording of inner or outer perception; it makes by words and music new possibilities of perceiving. Distinctive realms appear to us when we look and hear by poem-light. And these realms clearly are needed—there is no human culture that does not have its songs and poems.

One way we praise a work of art is to say it has "vision,"

and good poetry and good seeing go together almost always. Yet before art's more ground-level seeing can liberate itself into that other vision we speak of, a transfiguration is needed. The eyes and ears must learn to abandon the habits of useful serving and take up instead a participatory delight in their own ends. A work of art is not a piece of fruit lifted from a tree branch: it is a ripening collaboration of artist, receiver, and world.

A painter enacts perception's pleasure through brushstroke and color. For a poet, an equally material eros transforms the engagement with words. Consider, for example, the enkindled and sensuous seeing-through-language, hearing-through-language, to be found in Gerard Manley Hopkins. Even in prose, the voracious attention Hopkins gave to the shapes and forms of existence inhabits words precisely honed, originally tuned, and infused with the joy of category-leaping. Here is a journal entry from February 24, 1873:

> In the snow[,] flat-topped hillocks and shoulders outlined with wavy edges, ridge below ridge, very like the grain of wood in line and in projection like relief maps. These the wind makes I think and of course drifts, which are in fact snow waves. The sharp nape of a drift is sometimes broken by slant flutes or channels. I think this must be when the wind after shaping the drift first has changed and cast waves in the body of the wave itself. All the world is full of inscape and chance left free to act falls into an order as well as purpose: looking out of my window I caught it in the

random clods and broken heaps of snow made by the cast of a broom. The same of the path trenched by footsteps in ankledeep snow across the fields leading to Hodder wood through which we went to see the river.

Intimate, physically engaged, this account awakens both senses and psyche. Consider "the sharp nape of a drift"— how the word choice surprises by tenderness, as if Hopkins had reached out to touch the snow and found it humanly warm. In the equally physical "trenched by footsteps," we not only see but hear the snow re-made by our human passage through it. Flutes, shoulders, wood grain, maps, waves—each bounds with the exhilaration of seeing made monarch, not slave.

And more: the snow is further inquired of, investigated for what ideas it might yield. Hopkins's mid-passage insight is startlingly contemporary. "Chance left free to act falls into an order as well as purpose" is a sentence with which current complexity theorists might well agree. Then, having struck this spark of abstraction from his snow-chilled flint, Hopkins's thoughts do what the thoughts of poets do: return to the realm of things, for test and confirmation. He comes back to what the snow looks like, broom-swept from the front door: an image that visually rhymes with, and so verifies, the idea he has found in the natural realm. The passage, like many other descriptive entries in Hopkins's journals, could only have been written by a person in love with close observation, one who sees with the whole body, and also with the senses of emotion and mind.

But then, there is this:

As kingfishers catch fire, dragonflies draw flame;
As tumbled over rim in roundy wells
Stones ring; like each tucked string tells, each hung bell's
Bow swung finds tongue to fling out broad its name;

And this:

I caught this morning morning's minion,
kingdom of daylight's dauphin, dapple-dawn-drawn Falcon, in his
*   riding*
Of the rolling level underneath him steady air . . .

And this:

Earnest, earthless, equal, attuneable, | vaulty, voluminous, . . .
*   stupendous*
Evening strains to be time's vast, | womb-of-all, home-of-all,
*   hearse-of-all night.*
Her fond yellow hornlight wound to the west, | her wild
*   hollow hoarlight hung to the height*
Waste; her earliest stars, earlstars, | stars principal, overbend us,
Fire-featuring heaven.

The gap between the voice of Hopkins's journal and the voice of his poems isn't simply the difference between rough diary-jotting and finished work, or the difference between prose and verse. It is the difference between a poet's seeing and *poetry*'s seeing, and hearing, speech. One may help make the other possible, but they are not the same, in kind or intention—and the distinction exists because poetry itself, when allowed to, becomes within us a playable organ of perception, sounding out its own forms of knowledge and forms of discovery. Poems do not simply express. They make, they find, they sound (in both meanings of that word) things undiscoverable by other means. "Earlstars," "daylight's dauphin," even the seemingly simple description of "roundy wells"—each is a note newly made, on a keyboard expanded to hold its presence.

Hopkins's work is one of the great exemplars we have of poetry's expansion of accurate knowing. The idiosyncratic marriage of vision and ear in his poems unlocked the forms of English verse; a perception emanating from the passion for words sprung fully to music lies somewhere close to the marrow of his genius. Hopkins's desire for a wellspring seeing peeled his mind, tongue, and ear free of convention. The resulting permeability to whatever comes forward, however "counter" or strange, sustains the fierce aliveness found in even the darkest of his works. Seeing through poetry's eyes, hearing through poetry's ears, we come to know ourselves less tempered, more free than we were, and connected to— emancipated into, if you will—a larger world.

> *Not, I'll not, carrion comfort, Despair, not feast on thee;*
> *Not untwist—slack they may be—these last strands of man*
> *In me or, most weary cry* I can no more. I can;
> *Can something, hope, wish day come, not choose not to be.*

The quiet, declarative "I can" of Hopkins's "Carrion Comfort" carries a promise: the commitment to full experience is an infusion and elixir that works against whatever diminishes the soul, even despair. Oxygen is available; so long as the poet is speaking, it can be breathed.

∽

There are ways of sensing beyond our familiar litany of sight, hearing, taste, smell, and touch. Fish have an organ, the lateral line, running the length of the body, with which they sense not only vibrations in the water but also depth, direction, and temperature. Carrier pigeons use vision to navigate and yet, set free hooded, will still find their way home, following the currents of the earth's magnetic fields. A bean plant has no nervous system, no eyes or fingertips, yet turns, hour by hour, toward the sun; a clematis ignored for a decade will—at last given a spring trellis to climb— shoot up five feet in three weeks.

In the last instants of a shark's approach to its prey, it closes its inner eyelids for self-protection, and most of its other senses shut down as well. Only one remains active: a bioelectrical sensory mechanism in its jaw, a guidance system uniquely made for striking. The poet in the heat of writing is a bit like that shark, perceiving in ways unique to the moment of imminent connection.

Poems appear, as often as not, to arise in looking outward: the writer turns toward the things of the world, sees its kingfishers and falcons, hears the bells of churches and sheep, and these outer phenomena seem to give off meaning almost as if a radiant heat. But the heat is in us, of course, not in things. During writing, in the moment an idea arrives, the eyes of ordinary seeing close down and the poem rushes forward into the world on some mysterious inner impulsion that underlies seeing, underlies hearing, underlies words as they exist in ordinary usage. The condition is almost sexual, procreative in its hunger for what can be known no other way. All writers recognize this surge of striking; in its energies the objects of the world are made new, alchemized by their passage through the imaginal, musical, world-foraging and word-forging mind.

This altered vision is the secret happiness of poems, of poets. It is as if the poem encounters the world and finds in it a hidden language, a Braille unreadable except when raised by the awakened imaginative mind. Hopkins's kingfisher is both a kingfisher and more than a kingfisher; his rung bell travels equally through the tunnels of spirit and ear. The inward life spills into material substances, fragrances, and sounds, as material substances, fragrance, and sound spill into each other. This double life of objects is at work in a traditional Japanese haiku, an Australian aboriginal chant, a Nahuatl flower song, a twenty-first-century American experimental lyric. Finding ourselves in the realm of poetic perception, we return to the word's first conception: poïesis as *making*.

To say it outright: a poem is not the outer event or phenomenon it ostensibly describes, nor is it the feeling or insight it may seem to reveal or evoke. A poem may involve both, but is, more complexly, a living fabrication of new comprehension—"fabrication" meaning, not accidentally, both "lie," "falsehood," and, more simply and fundamentally, anything created and made: the bringing of something freshly into being. Fabric, whether of material or mind, is an interwoven invention: some substance—silk or cotton, wool or image—made stronger, larger than itself, by the dual-natured meeting of warp thread and weft thread. A work of art holds our lives as they are known when fully engaged with the multiple, crossing experience-strands of self, language, culture, emotion, senses, and mind.

What gives poetry's threads their hold and tensile power to discover is music. Take even one line of Hopkins's poetry, attending purely to its sound, and you can see clearly the braided, musical making that draws its parts into a larger and enlarging whole. "As kingfishers catch fire, dragonflies draw flame"—the line flares a copulant beauty. In its first half, the "k" of "kingfishers" repeats itself in the hard "c" of "catch," while its mid-word "f" returns in "fire." An identical pattern is hand-tied, as if in the way a fisherman's fly is, into the following phrase: the opening consonants of "dragonflies" repeat in "draw," its middle dipthong returns in "flame." The vowels, too, confirm the strengthening of recurrence: the "i" in "kingfishers" repeats in "fire," the "a" of "dragonflies" in "flame," each shifting from short to long in pronunciation. We cannot always know whether such intricate sound work is made by conscious effort or by some less deliberate, more intuitive process. What matters is that things are said, are seen, in the ways of connection and enlargement, when said and seen in the ways of poems.

Poetry's generative power, then, lies not in its "message" or "meaning," nor in any simple recording of something external to its own essence. It resides within the palace of its own world-embedded, intertwining existence. Poems speak in a language invented by mixed and untethered modes of perception, in grammars and textures that instruct first writer, then reader, in how to see, hear, and feel through poetry's own senses and terms. Those terms include the communicative elements of content, craft, and form. They include also a certain kind of tropism—poems lean toward increase of meaning, feeling, and being.

.

But how does the writer, poetry's amanuensis, rise to meet this yearning for increase? Surely he or she brings to the page not only what is already known but also the contrapuntal impulse of a permeable intention. The writing of poems must be counted as much a contemplative practice as a communicative one, and in the contemplative byways of every tradition, a reshaped intention is the ground of change. By intention's ripening, the thirteenth-century Japanese Zen teacher Eihei Dogen said, the white milk of rivers grows fragrant and sweet—a statement only comprehensible to the ears and mind awake also to the transformative language of poems. Intention welcomes the new less by force of effort than by dissolving the psyche's old habits, gestures, forms. It is the enactment of an invitation to something that does not yet exist.

The kind of intention I speak of here is not the kind referred to in courts of law: contemplative intention is translucent to what lies beyond the self. Will and choice may play a role, but creative intention's heightened speech requires an equally intensified listening, as a violinist must listen to orchestra, violin, and body if he or she is to play well. The listening goes into the violin's sound as much as the drawing of the bow across the strings. A similar transformation occurs when a person sits down within the intentions of poetry. Poetry's addition to our lives takes place in the border realm where inner and outer, actual and possible, experienced and imaginable, heard and silent, meet. The gift of poetry is that its seeing is not our usual seeing, its hearing is not our usual hearing, its knowing is not our usual knowing, its will is not our usual will. In a poem, everything travels both inward and outward.

In *shikantaza,* the form of Zen meditation practiced by Dogen, a person's eyes are neither fully closed nor fully open: they are held in a state of betweenness. A similar gaze, lowered yet present, is called by Catholic monastics "keeping custody of the eyes." Neither escape, disregard, nor avoidance, this careful balancing of attention's direction reflects an altered expectation of what is being looked for. The desire of monks and mystics is not unlike that of artists: to perceive the extraordinary within the ordinary by changing not the world but the eyes that look. Within a summoned and hybrid awareness, the inner reaches out to transform the outer, and the outer reaches back to transform the one who sees. Catherine of Siena wrote, in the fourteenth century, "All the way to heaven is heaven"; Marcel Duchamp, in the third year of the First World War, submitted a porcelain urinal to an art show, titling it *Fountain.* Both say: to form the intention of new awareness is already to transform and be transformed.

Is it possible to say that poetry's seeing is both innate and learned? Even the ordinary vision we are born with is learned. We know this from studies of the congenitally blind: after surgery makes possible the physical capacity to see, there remains a lag in cognition, in the ability to parse image from sensory data. One eight-year-old boy, operated on in the early 1900s for cataracts, was asked, when his bandages were first removed, what he could see. "I don't know," he answered. The surgeon moved his hand in front of the boy, who still could "see" nothing. Only after the boy touched the moving hand with his own did he begin to recognize the shifting patterns of light and dark before him for what they were.

Our simplest acts of perception depend, then, upon an experiential and experimentally crafted knowledge. Perception is not passively given us; it is a continually expanding interaction and engagement, both mental and physical, with the world. Sound, temperature, motion enter the attention of an infant even before birth, and that cog-and-wheel conversation continues until the moment of death. A parallel process unfolds in the making of art. What a writer or painter undertakes in each work of art is an experiment whose hoped-for outcome is an expanded knowing. Each gesture, each failed or less-than-failed attempt to create an experience by language or color and paper, is imagination reaching outward to sieve the world. To make a genuine work of art, or even to take in such a work fully, is to tie a further knot on that fisherman's intricate fly.

But there is more: it is as if the fish of perception did not exist until it is caught. The physicist Arthur Zajonc once designed what he called a "box of light." In it, a bright projector casts light into a space in which no surface or object is visible. When the viewer looks inside, what is seen appears to be absolute darkness. Then the person is shown how to move a handle on the side of the box, to control a movable wand—and once an object is brought into the space, it is clear that a brilliance falls onto it from one direction, and that the other side is in shadow. Light, as the experiment was designed to show, is only perceptible when it catches upon the stuff of the world. Or, more precisely, it is only perceptible to us when three elements are present: when the looking mind catches light entangled in the net of things.

Consider three words: "apprehend," "comprehend," "prehensile." There is, deep in the process of human knowing, a necessary and active reaching out—to understand is to *grasp*, to *take in*. The philosophers of ancient Greece believed that vision was a beam thrown out by the eyes as if from a lantern. Like the boy who could not see a hand until he himself had touched it, the mind, before it can enter a new perception, needs first to extend itself into existence in tangible ways. Poetic imagination is muscular, handed, and kinesthetic. The tongue, the ear, the eye, the alertness of skin, entwine the world for which and by which they come into being, and of which each is part. In its musics, its objects, its strategies of speech, thought, and feeling, a poem plucks the interconnection of the experiencing self and all being. In poetry's words, life calls to life with the same inevitability and gladness that bird calls to bird, whale to whale, frog to frog. Listening across the night or ocean or pond, they recognize one another and are warmed by that knowledge.

There is no way to convey this prehensile imagination and its liberating reach, except by example. Hopkins is filled with that heat of connection. Here are a few other fragments charged with imaginative transference, by more recent poets.

> *The fish are dreadful. They are brought up*
> *the mountain in the dawn most days, beautiful*
> *and alien and cold from night under the sea,*
> *the grand rooms fading from their flat eyes.*
> Soft machinery of the dark, *the man thinks,*
> *washing them.*

> Jack Gilbert, from "Going Wrong"

> *One was a bay cowhorse from Piedra & the other was a washed-out*
> *   palomino*
> *And both stood at the rail of the corral & both went on aging*
> *In each effortless tail swish, the flies rising, then congregating again*

> *Around their eyes & muzzles & withers.*

> *Their front teeth were by now yellow as antique piano keys & slanted*
> *   to the angle*
> *Of shingles on the maze of sheds & barn around them; their puckered*

*Chins were round & black as frostbitten oranges hanging unpicked
    from the limbs
Of trees all through winter like a comment of winter itself on
    everything
That led to it & found gradually the way out again.*

*In the slowness of time. Black time to white, & rind to blossom.
Deity is in the details & we are details among other details & we long
    to be*

Teased out of ourselves. And become all of them.

Larry Levis, from "Elegy with a Bridle in Its Hand"

The ache of marriage;

*thigh and tongue, beloved,
are heavy with it,
it throbs in the teeth*

Denise Levertov, from "The Ache of Marriage"

*Lay down these words
Before your mind like rocks.
    placed solid, by hands
In choice of place, set
Before the body of the mind
    in space and time:
Solidity of bark, leaf, or wall
    riprap of things:*

Cobble of milky way,
    straying planet

Gary Snyder, from "Riprap"

Back, behind us,
the dignified tall firs begin.
Bluish, associating with their shadows,
a million Christmas trees stand
waiting for Christmas. The water seems suspended
above the rounded gray and blue-gray stones.
I have seen it over and over, the same sea, the same,
slightly, indifferently swinging above the stones,
icily free above the stones,
above the stones and then the world.
If you should dip your hand in,
your wrist would ache immediately,
your bones would begin to ache and your hand would burn
as if the water were a transmutation of fire
that feeds on stones and burns with a dark gray flame.

Elizabeth Bishop, from "At the Fishhouses"

In his *Rhetoric*, Aristotle praises what he calls "active metaphor" for the quickening it brings to the reader's mind. He especially notes the way Homer endows the inanimate with life, using as his example a description of spears "standing fast in the ground, though longing to feed on flesh." Aristotle uses the term "metaphor" broadly, to signal any attributive transference; current usage might name his example "personification" or call it Ruskin's "pathetic fallacy"—attributing feeling to objects. But the essential observation holds: poetic perception inhabits an animate world, infused with empathic connection. Qualities human or animal spring forth from seemingly stolid objects. Attributes belonging to one being or thing phosphoresce inside another. Shape-shifting, metamorphosis, transmutation: these are the leavenings of thought, the yeast and heat by which flour and water rise into sweet-scented bread.

Metaphoric transformation is not the sole means of poetic imagination—there is the cello's singing made purely by sound craft, there are the muscles and hinged joints of story, the sinew of abstract statement, the footfall of a single, awakening image standing in its own thrown light. But kaleidoscopic mind—whether flamboyant or subtle—is one marker for the poet reaching actively toward a renewing perception. From the work of Hopkins, and each of the writers presented here, springs a supple, turning aliveness, the hawk's-swoop voracity of the mind when it is both precise and free. Different as they are, there is something entirely unshackled in each of these poets. You feel they could say anything, from within the liberated energies of creative seeing.

Consider Jack Gilbert's fish, whose flat eyes hold grand, fading rooms. (Here I pause to imagine Aristotle's pleasure in the active motion of that present-participial "fading.") To find such wholly surprising rooms—the plural, too, is important—vanishing inside the eyes of the fish plunges the writer, the reader, into his or her own multichambered sense of the possible. We pursue that receding image through interior passageways, doors beyond doors. Calling the skeleton "soft machinery of the dark," Gilbert enlarges the fish further still—in the phrase, three quite different image systems (tactile softness; darkness both visual and inner; technological gleam of machine) come quietly together, with the slight, almost silent tock of a lock's tumblers slipping into alignment before it falls open. These fish will become, over the course of the poem, a kind of metonym: gutted and deboned on the table, they signal the sustenance the poet eats, containing, as he goes on to say, "the muck of something terrible." They are also the sustenance of poetry, whose flesh and blood and intricate machinery carry Gilbert, and us, forward, fully fed within the austerity he has also chosen.

The liberating transformation in Larry Levis's passage has to do with time, as it is tracked through a procession of shifting objects: time is counted on the metronome of tail-swish, it yellows into teeth like old piano keys, it tastes of frostbitten, unpicked oranges. Each new image steps cleanly into the arc—and ark—of the poem. Each seems inevitable as soon as it's met. Yet who before Levis has seen frostbitten oranges in the underchins of old horses? And then, like a field of ten thousand blossoms reduced to an eighth ounce of essential oil, come the time-reversing words, "In the slowness of time. Black time to white, & rind to blossom," before the poem returns to chronicling the beloved lost.

In Denise Levertov's poem, the realm-transferring image, strong as a physical blow, is marriage throbbing in the teeth—her phrase shows that what is made first by ritual must be lived out deep in the body, in all of its parts: the grinding, subliminally violent jaw is present within any kiss.

Gary Snyder, from the early "Riprap" to his most recent work, has been our practitioner of the manual imagination. Others have laid trail, felled trees, rebuilt engines, and learned the names of rock, but he is the one who showed American poets how to make these activities *see*. "Cobble of milky way" is a conjunction only a poet who has worked stones could have made.

Finally, there is Elizabeth Bishop, whose closely considered objects shift continually into new life. Dignity, patient expectancy, indifference—all these human attributes are placed into fir tree and ocean with a seamless, unsentimental ease, and the objects and elements under her gaze transform, one into another, with equal ease. In the lines shown here, the transformation takes place explicitly through the mediating human—it is by a hand dipped into icy waters that saltwater turns into fire.

I have called this transubstantiation of being the secret happiness of poems, of poets: secret because rarely spoken of, and secret, too, because even the poets themselves often fail to recognize the source of their own joy in writing, or even joy's presence as the pen leaps to enact it. No matter how difficult the subject, while writing, a poet is unchained from sadness, and free. The means of this unlatching is a theme that will run throughout this book.

Ovid's *Metamorphoses* holds many explicit accountings of the soul's love of changing. In subtler ways, any good work of art embodies a version its own and no other's. The change of key in a piece of music; the downward and inward gaze in Piero della Francesca's *Madonna del Parto*— we need only look, and some sense of turning is there to be found.

To close, here again is Hopkins—this time a poem in its entirety.

MOONRISE JUNE 19 1876

I awoke in the midsummer not-to-call night, | in the white and the walk of the morning:

The moon, dwindled and thinned to the fringe | of a fingernail held to the candle,

Or paring of paradisiacal fruit, lovely in waning but lustreless,

Stepped from the stool, drew back from the barrow, | of dark Manaefa the mountain;

A cusp still clasped him, a fluke yet fanged him, | entangled him, not quit utterly.

This was the prized, the desireable sight, | unsought, presented so easily,

Parted me leaf and leaf, divided me, | eyelid and eyelid of slumber.

Gerard Manley Hopkins

Among the range of Hopkins's work one might call this a sketch—unrhymed, a little unripe somehow, quite possibly an abandoned start. And still, what overspilling density it holds, seeing as it does with poetry's eyes. The moon named as a "paring of paradisiacal fruit" is a moon almost fragrant to the imagination; the "white and the walk of the morning" is an unparsable phrase, making perfected alliterative equals of color and action. The poem, too, raises a thought I have increasingly come to believe holds true: that good description in poetry is never purely description, it is a portrait of a state of being, of soul.

For me, though, this poem's last two lines are the richest treasure; the first for the knowledge that the prize of vision arrives unsought, as grace, while our more purposeful consciousness sleeps; and the second for its luminous intertwining of inner and outer: "Parted me leaf and leaf, divided me, | eyelid and eyelid of slumber." No matter how many times I read these words I am left uncertain, sound-spelled, placed into the sleepy wonderment of a young child: Is it the poet awakened by this slim remnant of mountain-held moon, or is it the leafy world itself that awakens, in the poem's own moon-opened eyes?

CHAPTER TWO

Language Wakes Up in the Morning: On Poetry's Speaking

L anguage wakes up in the morning. It has not yet washed its face, brushed its teeth, combed its hair. It does not remember whether or not, in the night, any dreams came. The light is the plain light of day, indirect— the window faces north—but strong enough to see by nonetheless.

Language goes to the tall mirror that hangs on one wall and stands before it, wearing no makeup, no slippers, no robe. In the same circumstances, we might see first our two eyes, looking back at their own inquiring. We might glance down to the two legs on which vision stands. What language sees in the mirror is also twofold—the two foundation powers of image and statement. The first foundation, image, holds the primary, wordless world of the actual, its heaped assemblage of quartzite, feathers, steel trusses, red-seamed baseballs, distant airplanes, and a few loudly complaining cows, traveling from every direction into the self's interior awareness. The second foundation, state-ment, is our human answer, traveling outward back into the world—our stories, our theories, our judgments, our epics and lyrics and work songs, birth notices and epitaphs, newspaper articles and wedding invitations, the infinite coherence-makings of form. All that is sayable begins with these two modes of attention and their prolific offspring. Begins, that is, with the givens of experienced, embodied existence and the responses we offer the world in return.

"Image": The word comes from the Latin *imago,* a "pic-ture" or "likeness." An image is not the primary world, though that is its source. It is the constellated, partitioned understanding we frame and know that world by, once it has come into the mind. Once formed, an image of a crow at dusk or a shopping mall storefront, of a pencil or a factory floor thick-bolted with pounding machinery, may remain in the possibility-storehouse of imagination; or it may travel back into the outer world in the form of paint or stone or word.

Some images enter the mind by touch, others are heard or seen. Some are simple, others complex. Here is a simple image: a small fish hovers in a creek, its body exactly the color and variegation of the algae-draped rocks below it. For an instant, the onlooker rests only in noticing that. But it is not mind's nature to stop with what it first sees. The mind goes on to observe that in its streaked camouflage mottling, the fish—it is a young trout—appears to be itself a rock, but a rock drifting somehow, and a little transpar-ent. It appears to be what a rock would be if a rock could dream itself alive. Then perhaps comes the memory of having seen this before. Generations of trout have made a home in the same deep place in the streambed, scooped to steepness by ten thousand years of winter rains; the watcher recalls having seen more than a few. Then the mind continues further: "Almost big enough to eat," the mind murmurs. "Two good mouthfuls, if I were truly hungry."

Our human attention has many ways of engaging the primary world in any moment—perception, identification, comparison, associative drift, memory, the attraction/aversion of fear and desire, the old evaluative habits of predator in the presence of prey. And somewhere in their midst, image-mind becomes the mind of statement—the rock of pure being breaks free from its creek bed mooring in the world and swims off: lithe, muscled, and hungry for what the world tastes of, for what it can make use of, play with, mate. Little splinter of life force looking for something to do, because that is its nature.

As a horse crops grass or a pear tree makes pears, we make statements. They come in different forms—some are propositions, some are suppositions, some are narratives; some are similes, recipes, questions. All are ways we cross more fully into being, plunge into a reciprocal engagement with the scouring, altering outer. Looked at from its own word-history, a statement is how we declare our place in the world. The word's Indo-European root leads back to "stand"—holding oneself upright on the earth. Standing is the human posture in the body, and statement the human posture in the mind. Its cognates are many, and illuminative. At their heart is the pause of the Greek word *stasis:* something sufficiently stopped to be physically or mentally weighed. To stare, for instance, requires a stillness of both subject and object: we must be able to look both deeply and long. The root holds also an aspect of display—the stand we put under a statue; a theater's raised and lit stage. The arranging of standing things to be examined becomes, in late Latin, the concept of system. "Stanza," at first meaning a "dwelling," later becomes one of the separate but adjacent rooms in which the parts of a poem reside. The route from "stationary," unmoving, to "stationery," the paper carrying words meant to travel, goes straight through a bookseller's stall in the Roman market. And finally, the verb "to state" refers originally to fixing a thought or object into its detailed particularity, in order to express its definitive condition, its "state" (now noun) of being. All these etymologies point toward an intimate connection between considered language and contemplative pause, meaning wrested from the rush of precipitate experience by the addition of time.

·

But the mind does not remain rooted in any one statement; it, too, moves ceaselessly from one state to the next. One of the ways it does this is by musing—no accident, that word used to describe the ways in which thought's more fluid transformations occur. "To muse" implies entering a condition of idleness, outside the responsibilities of the fully adult: a playfulness marks the self-amusing, musing mind. It lifts a thing, turns it over, licks it, sees if it moves; explores in a way that leaves behind both simple preconception and the directionality of strict purpose. Here, too, etymology reveals. "Muse" derives from the Latin *mussare,* meaning first "to carry in silence," then "to brood over in silence and uncertainty," and then only finally "to murmur or mutter, to speak in an undertone." Musing, it seems, is a thing that happens best in the circumstances of quiet. Undogmatic and tactful before the object of its attention, musing does not impose, but bears witness. It quietly considers, and then, when it finally speaks, does so with the voice, respectful of other presences, that we use in a library, church, or museum—the voice used, that is, when we feel we are in the company of something more important than ourselves. The mind that muses is modest and un-insistent, permeable to what lies beyond comprehension, amenable to some sense of proportion and the comic. Arrogance reserves itself for the more self-involved.

Within the word "muse" reside also, of course, the nine Greek figures of Helicon—Erato, Euterpe, Terpsichore, Polyhymnia, Clio, Calliope, Melpomene, Thalia, Urania. Hesiod calls them the daughters of Earth and Air; others say they were begotten during the nine nights Zeus spent with Mnemosyne, goddess of Memory. Between them the moods and curiosities of human existence are hummed: the stories of historical narrative and epic wanderings; the poems of eros and feeling and landscape; the irreducible buoyancies of music, dance, and laughter; the cautions of tragedy's examples; the answers we make to the sacred; the questions we ask in awe of the shining stars.

The nine sister Muses are depicted always as virginal, young. Perhaps their youthfulness carries the silence, the doubt, of *mussare*'s first meanings. The very young animal, when it is learning, begins by watching, by listening, by testing, by taking in. Then it experiments with its body, its tongue, its desires. It is neither self-conscious nor contained. And what is virgin does not yet know, and so stays open. The Muses, in their slender and untested forms, remain strangely unwetted by the enormous floodwaters of creation that pass through their beings. An epic, a tragedy, a concerto, is finished, and the next begins as it must: from the silence preceding beginning, from the condition where nothing as yet exists—not the first word, not the first note, not key or tempo, gesture or subject. Only a template is there, or perhaps even less: a proclivity. This is why the Muses do not age. Only in the realm of the human, earthly existence does knowledge transform the body.

A poem by the Swedish poet and novelist Lars Gustafsson captures the condition of the world as the Muses might know it before they have changed it by their own workings—a world purely image, in which the mind-created realm of statement scarcely exists:

THE STILLNESS OF THE WORLD BEFORE BACH

There must have been a world before
the Trio Sonata in D, a world before the A minor Partita,
but what kind of a world?
A Europe of vast empty spaces, unresounding,
everywhere unawakened instruments
where the Musical Offering, *the* Well-Tempered Clavier
never passed across the keys.
Isolated churches
where the soprano line of the Passion

never in helpless love twined round
the gentler movements of the flute,
broad soft landscapes
where nothing breaks the stillness
but old woodcutters' axes,
the healthy barking of strong dogs in winter
and, like a bell, skates biting into fresh ice;
the swallows whirring through summer air,
the shell resounding at the child's ear
and nowhere Bach nowhere Bach
the world in a skater's stillness before Bach.

Lars Gustafsson
tr. by Philip Martin

The landscape of Gustafsson's pre-Bach world—a world into which art's disruptions and re-constellations have not yet come—is a country of childhood and fairy-tale innocence, one preceding the complications of adult knowledge. Archetype has not yet been stamped by its own emergence. Daughters of memory, the Muses remember form, remember pattern, remember an arc of awakening and the sleep that follows, but content—even content as transformative as the music of Bach—passes tracelessly through them. Their gaze is always turned toward the not-yet-imagined.

∼

Let us return to the morning bedroom, to the moment when language awakens to rise, looks outward, looks inward, asks its one question: "What might I say?" What does it mean when the answer arrives through the gate of a Muse, arrives, that is, in the form we think of as art?

Thought is thought, color is color, sound is sound. Each becomes recognizable also as art when a secondary awareness, one tuned toward shapeliness, movement, and intention, enters in. The forms we experience as "art" balance between the stilled familiarity of established knowledge and the fluidity of the creative mind at play. The linguistic root of "art" means most simply "skill": it signals a task undertaken in some particularly effective way. Near it in the dictionary are words concerning themselves with small, ingenious, and movable fittings: words used to denote the body's physical joints, or the idea of compression, or the condition of things packed tightly together while still maintaining their distinctness. Etymologically, then, an "articulate" person is one who speaks by dividing things into their precise parts, but also with awareness of the precisely geared clockworks on which an argument must turn. The "artificial" is that which has been cleverly maneuvered, altered by the ingenious human hand. The artist begins by fitting one thing into another—a cup to its hand, a lid to its box, a color to its image, a story to its cultural and individual occasion. Once placed into the world, the cup is lifted for use, the lid swivels on its small brass hinges, the story shifts a little with each telling.

A good poem, though, goes beyond its own well-madeness. Even in motionless, time-fixed paintings and sculpture, there is the feeling of hinge-turn we find in poems and often name with the terms of music—alterations of rhythm or key that raise alterations of comprehension and mood. Music, almost undefinable in itself, is delineated by philologists by contrasting it not to silence but to "noise"—sound that lacks structure, intention, and meaning. Music's self-aware re-orderings bring experience out of randomness and into the arc of shaping direction, into the cross-trusses of what has been made recognizably formal. These shifts are made by patterned departure and return, by dramatic selection, by awareness of cadence shift, emphasis, harmony and useful dissonance—all the progressive unfoldings of sound-rhyme and sound-variation we have come to find useful engagements with feeling and beauty. Language enters artfulness by the same means. But ordinary language, unlike ordinary noise, does already include structure, purpose, and meaning. One way language signals its entrance to art, then, is by the inclusion of music's intensified awareness and music's full-ranging, engaging intentions. The sentences of poetry, fiction, drama, attend to their music the way a tree attends to its leaves: motile and many, seemingly discardable, they remain the sustenance-source by which it lives.

The centrality of movement and alteration in any art form can be seen by what happens if the word "art" is given a negative prefix: the opposite of art is inertness. It is the nature of living beings to move—some quickly as that stream-immersed trout when an insect disturbs the surface above it, others as slowly and inexorably as a bishop pine growing the narrowest of annual rings around its two-thousand-year-old heartwood. Art—some part of a life distilled to essential and self-aware gesture—is similarly active and moving, in its enactments and in its effects. And when a work of art is unable to move us—because of some failure in its conception or clumsiness of execution, or because we are too far from its originating circumstances to understand what request it makes of the senses, heart, and mind—that work itself becomes inert, becomes noise, deafened to meaning and feeling.

Art that keeps its heat and breath is quick, alive as a blow. Consider the force of this late, margin-scrawled fragment by Keats. Not finished, not shapely, deeply uncharacteristic, it has preserved nonetheless a place among his most-known poems:

> *This living hand, now warm and capable*
> *Of earnest grasping, would, if it were cold*
> *And in the icy silence of the tomb,*
> *So haunt thy days and chill thy dreaming nights*
> *That thou would wish thine own heart dry of blood,*
> *So in my veins red life might stream again,*
> *And thou be conscience-calm'd. See, here it is—*
> *I hold it towards you.*

John Keats

The heat of life and the ice of death coincide in this poem. The request and implied threat of its words are, in one way of reading them, shocking—but the reader's ethical response depends upon where in time the poem is placed in his or her mind. Are these words spoken by the living man to his beloved, or from the grave? The grammar and facts of its composition tell us we must see it as the former; yet the poem's concluding statement cannot help but now be heard in the second way—these words come to us from beneath the shroud. Read in this posthumous and proleptic way, we can forgive their proposition of desperate exchange: their speaker knows it impossible. Still, we should not read these lines for anything less brutal than they are, nor lightly pass over that fact, however heartbreaking we may also find them. "I want to live," the poem says, "and I would take your life-blood if I could in order to do it." It offers an unveiled depiction of the way the artist occupies the psyche of others. Aspiring to the immediacy of life, art is rapacious to escape the laws of human transience.

As we saw in looking at Gerard Manley Hopkins, art's shapeliness baits not only time, but thought itself. Patterned and musical, awake to its own voice, compressive, heightening, any work of art that is not superficial is more than a stylized outward signaling. Art's desire is not to convey the already established but to transform the life that takes place within its presence. Understanding grows resonant and amplified, as certain plants grow more fragrant in the warmth of the late afternoon, or as an ant surrounded by amber becomes more than simply the relic of an ancient insect. Quickened as well as stilled, the ant is kept in the gesture of its single moment, one leg raised in the attitude of escape. In the suddenness and completeness of its enclosure is the tension between living subject and preservation. The viewer recognizes the same tension in certain Chinese scrolls and Renaissance sculptures. Even the forty-thousand-year old bison of Lascaux seem to shift on their cave walls in the light of a raised-up torch. What is trapped in and by artfulness grows dense, in both habitat and habitation: to enter a work of art is to enter a thicket. Caught itself, it then catches us. And then, equally, releases.

∽

Drop a leaf into water and it will simply be taken, sliding swiftly between rocks and away. But that small fish in the creek, living, both darts at will through the current and resists it. Just so, a work of art resists time while shaping itself to a form that can navigate and answer time's continual pressure. The alternations and returns of formal rhyme and meter are the most obvious outward means by which a poem combines movement and stillness to outwit time, but free verse's more subtle architectures accomplish the same end. We can see time netted in the structure of poems across centuries of aesthetic possibility-shifting. Consider the opening three lines of Robert Herrick's seventeenth-century love poem, "On Julia's Clothes":

Whenas in silks my Julia goes,
Then, then, methinks, how sweetly flows
That liquefaction of her clothes.

Now hear those of Louise Glück's more recent "Unwritten Law":

Interesting how we fall in love:
in my case absolutely. Absolutely, and, alas, often—
so it was in my youth.

The difference in diction, approach, sensibility, sound, is vast. Yet each poem is set in a non-standard form, and each engraves itself upon the mind of the reader by means of an audible shapeliness both exuberant and surely drawn.

Time's resistance, transformation, and remembrance form a large part of the reservoir of pleasure a good poem contains. And there is always pleasure, sometimes delicate and subterranean, sometimes a large-ribbed exulting. You can hear it in the excerpts just quoted: how each poem comes alive in the mouthing of its words. The rustling fabric of Herrick's consonants and vowels, the muscular wit not only of Glück's mind but of her music, are the means by which their lines' language-joy is taken in. This steady undercurrent of joy is the *elixir vitae* by which good art revives us, moistening the dry regions of more straightforward thought, more straightforward ways of seeing and hearing.

The existence of pleasure is as strong in art that addresses darkness as in that which unfolds by light, as present in the simple as in the complex. Why does plainness sometimes gleam, other times dull? Even in the world of the visual this is so—some colors saturate with richness and invite the eye, while others close their faces before us, and we in turn look elsewhere. Shaker tables and cupboards can be recognized by the hold they have on our eyes; art defines itself into being. We awaken into and by it, we are moved, altered, stirred. It may feel as if we have done nothing, only given a little time and space of attention; but some hairline-narrow crack opens in the self's sense of purpose, and there art, there beauty, is. The result is as irresistible as eros, as voracious as the new green weeds in the crack of a sidewalk. Art's limitlessness awakens in us the sense of the psyche's own limitless rooms. It is how the inner world grows continually new.

❧

What have we gathered thus far into our fold? The outer world of image in all its mottled shapes and scents, its antlered and stamened densities, its secretions of nectar and sweat. The complex or simple statements that are our reply to that world. The moods and modes of the gatekeeping Muses, their playfulness and also their silences, pauses, and doubts. The necessity for musical shapeliness and its muscular, resilient collaboration with time. Movement. The shivering joy of aesthetic encounter.

Next, perhaps, is experience, is knowledge. The Muses may be virginal, but a realized work requires both skills and materials. Its pieces must be found and fitted together, before it can bring into being the not-yet-known. For this, the sum of a life is needed. Everything we have lived and touched and learned from is the knowledge brought to the moment of creative making—emotional experiences, ethics, yearnings, heard bird calls and tasted breads, the storehouse of learning. A poet needs to know the parts of the internal combustion engine, the histories of Buenos Aires and the Ukraine, the fleeting trace-maps of particle physics, the poetries of South India, Portugal, and Iran. He or she needs to know the close to alchemical processes by which whiskey and honey come into being, the secret look that passes between mother and almost-grown son,

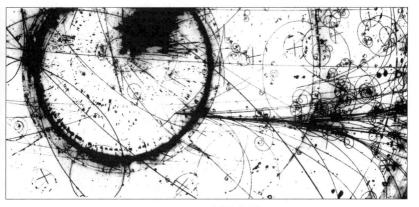

Neutrino event in bubble chamber

Detailed view of early
one-inch bubble chamber event

the narrow alleyways of rhetoric, the differing fatigues of failure and success. There is no way of telling in advance what part of our knowledge will be needed at any given moment. Hence, Henry James's apt formulation—the writer must be one on whom nothing is lost.

.

Seen from the point of view of art itself, the artist's life is not the source of the poem, the painting, the drama; it is its servant. Think of the beginning of a poem by Czesław Miłosz, "My Faithful Mother Tongue":

> *Faithful mother tongue,*
> *I have been serving you.*
> *Every night, I used to set before you little bowls of colors*
> *so you could have your birch, your cricket, your finch*
> *as preserved in my memory.*

But nothing in a good poem is simple, and the poet goes on:

> *This lasted many years.*
> *You were my native land; I lacked any other.*
> *I believed that you would also be a messenger*
> *between me and some good people*
> *even if they were few, twenty, ten*
> *or not born as yet.*
>
> *Now, I confess my doubt.*
> *There are moments when it seems to me I have squandered my life.*
> *For you are a tongue of the debased,*

of the unreasonable, hating themselves
even more than they hate other nations,
a tongue of informers,
a tongue of the confused,
ill with their own innocence.

But without you, who am I?
Only a scholar in a distant country,
a success, without fears and humiliations.
Yes, who am I without you?
Just a philosopher, like everyone else.

I understand, this is meant as my education:
the glory of individuality is taken away,
fortune spreads a red carpet
before the the sinner in a morality play
while on the linen backdrop a magic lantern throws
images of human and divine torture.

Faithful mother tongue,
perhaps after all it's I who must try to save you.
So I will continue to set before you little bowls of colors
bright and pure if possible,
for what is needed in misfortune is a little order and beauty.

Czesław Miłosz

translated by Czesław Miłosz and Robert Pinsky

This poem about the Polish language and the condition
of exile can be read as addressing also the place of poetry

itself in Miłosz's life. Poetry, too, is for Miłosz a mother tongue and an education, and it, too, he believed (as is clear from other of his writings) had been debased during his lifetime, put to frivolous, self-involved purposes, or wrong in ways more damaging yet. The convergence emerges from behind its curtain for an instant: surely it is without poetry, at least as much as without Polish, that Miłosz would be "just a philosopher, like everyone else"— merely another of the century's displaced persons caught in the examination of his own fate. Yet for a poet who continued through many decades of exile in first France, then America, to write his poems in Polish, it may be the two intertwined so thoroughly that they became one. Whether language is the poet's salvation or the poet is saving the language, the needed activity is the same—bowls of pure color are carried, simultaneously the material of making and a fragment of the incontrovertible Real.

Every good work of art holds something that was not quite knowable before its own existence. Sometimes the knowledge is investigated directly, as in Miłosz's lyric. Other times it is so subtle as to be almost imperceptible. There are poems, paintings, thoughts that rest in seeming silence a long time, like a turtle at rest on a creekside rock, unmoving but with its neck fully extended. It is hard to tell if its eyes are open or closed, until you move to just the right angle and all at once the sunlight glints in them. Then perhaps you can see: the turtle is watching you as well, from the alertness of its own particular life and being. Such knowledge is infinite and inexhaustible, as the world itself is infinite and inexhaustible—the writer need only look outward to see what looks back. One example of such a poem is D. H. Lawrence's "The White Horse." It is a "pansy," as Lawrence called his brief poetic versions of the French *pensée*—"a single thought, not an argument . . . true while they are true and irrelevant when the mood and circumstance changes."

THE WHITE HORSE

The youth walks up to the white horse, to put its halter on
and the horse looks at him in silence.
They are so silent they are in another world.

D. H. Lawrence

Almost nothing happens in this poem, and still it is oddly, strongly affecting. A moment of connection between two beings is described first from the outside, then, perhaps, from the inside. A simple image and act are accompanied by a single statement. What this poem knows seems as ungraspable as the knowledge that comes to us in a dream. And yet it meets Lawrence's requirement for a poetic "thought"—when we enter its words, a door is felt to open, and a light wind recognizably true blows through the reader. We step, with boy and horse, into a different world. It is the opening into an objective-seeming truth which gives poems of this kind, however slight they may appear to a casual glance, the weight of known life—as the rock-warmed turtle has actual weight, actual consequence, purely by the fact of its existence.

❦

In the realm of art, knowledge carries with it at all times an inevitable flavor—the individuality of the artist is in the work as the physical hands of the potter are in the clay, no matter how smoothed. It may be said this is true of all knowledge, that even a scientific calculation bears the marks of its human and social context. But in a work of art, the signs of personal sensibility are a part of what we look for: with a forensic pleasure in close perception, we distinguish one anonymous Old Master from the rest by the idiosyncratic pose of the hands, by the strange largeness and extra height of a woman's forehead.

Sensibility in a poem or painting reflects individuality back into the world of larger archetypes, impersonal forms, outward circumstances and currents. What the artist has been shaped by, moved by, soaked through with at some level deeper than consciousness or will, enters the poem as the edge of a metal printing press enters the paper. It is the touch of the actual meeting the actual: particularity's bite. In recent decades, the aesthetic of pure sensibility has risen to apparent ascendance. Sensibility has become so dominant a means by which metaphysics, psyche, politics, and emotional content are signaled that some artists and writers have tried in turn to erase it completely. Yet a recognizable style of vision and making is close to inescapable, as easily seen in the self-portraits of Rembrandt, the sonnets of Donne, and the haiku of Issa as in the work of Jean-Michel Basquiat, Wisława Szymborska, or John Ashbery. Within the most classical forms, there is more than sufficient play for a signature to calligraph itself into view; within modern aesthetic freedoms, "vision" and temperament become themselves the source for what Coleridge referred to as organic form.

Nor is sensibility a matter simply of syntax or of some characteristic emotional response—the capacious equanimity of Shakespeare before his characters is as fully a sensibility as any other. Keats's description of Shakespeare's genius as a negative capability, rather than a positive one, reminds us of Virgil's warning to Dante when traveling in hell: if he is to see rightly, pity is forbidden. The eye that wishes to see human nature complete must be unclouded by tears, unclouded even by allegiance. Pity, William Blake wrote, divides the soul.

For an artist, everything interests, instructs, is put to use. If we are to taste the full range of what is given art to carry, we will revel in Shakespeare's equanimity and also in works of partisan and partial genius: in Larkin's acerbic eye, Plath's rage, James Wright's or Neruda's harangues as well as their more permeably compassionate lyrics. Art carries all the flavors and scents of the human. The single, fundamental request of sensibility is that we respond in turn to what we perceive. As strong feeling initiates outer events, it initiates also art.

It was the Greek gods' pleasure, it seems, to stir up troubling passions; the working out of what then unfolded amused them. It also allowed them to partake of the range and weathers of human feeling, more interesting than their own eternal and essentially unchanging repetitions of stylized follies and feasts. In the human realm, what we make of our feelings matters: has weight, has breath, creates an irreversible fate. And so Antigone's millennia-old dilemma still moves us, and Orpheus's loss of Eurydice remains both the story of a heartbreaking surrender to human weakness and a clue—the true musician is the one who sings on, after the second loss. Even when music is powerless, even when it includes failure and shame as well as grief, he sings. Feeling what cannot be borne, he sings. Amidst and past his own dying, he sings. And that brings us to the last of what we will look at here.

.

Language has been up now for some time. It has showered, made a large pot of coffee, and drained the first blue mug. During the pause before pouring another, it has stepped into some clothes. Having no pressing, practical obligations to attend to, it is almost ready to go to the desk, to begin whatever work the morning may bring. There is one thing more, though, before it is ready—a demand without which language might never go to that awkward, armless, upright chair with its three wheeled feet; might instead lie on the couch and entertain itself with a good mystery, or perhaps step out into the garden and weed, since the day is opening into something warm and fine. The last thing language must know before the day's work begins is the burr of discomfort.

Dukka: the Sanskrit word appears in the first of the four noble truths of Buddhist teaching. Often translated as "suffering," its original meaning is closer to "dissatisfaction." "Life is dissatisfaction"—from this first observation and statement, the rest of the Buddhist path comes forward. Without dissatisfaction and suffering, there would be no path, no necessity for a path. For that reason, in Greek tragedies, in Trickster tales, in early epics and contemporary novels, in both Eastern and Western spiritual traditions, suffering is felt to be "noble," not a problem to be slipped away from or forgotten. It is by suffering's presence that we know there is something we need to address. And without some restless or inescapable dissatisfaction, why would a person spend a life setting one word and not another on a white page?

Surely the maker of a poem is never a comfortable and purely detached observer. The writer is driven, goaded, hounded. A letter Rilke sent to his wife makes his sense of extremity clear: a work of art, he wrote, is the outcome of "having-been-in-danger." For Rilke, as for many others, the central goad was transience, finding some way to take in and navigate the unbearable knowledge that life will end. In another letter, sent to his Polish translator, he wrote, "It is our task to imprint this provisional, perishing earth in ourselves so deeply, with such passion and endurance, that its reality rises again in us 'invisibly.' We are the bees of the invisible. We distractedly plunder the honey of the visible in order to gather it into the great golden hive of the Invisible" *(tr. by Jim Powell)*.

The resplendence and longing here are held within images of the earthly, yet this passage sets forth a fundamentally Platonic worldview: the (uppercase, conceptual) Invisible is the thing that lasts, while the actualities of earth exist for the sake of transformative plundering.

The description is irresistible, moving—and anthropocentrically pitched toward the transcendent. But what maker of art who works in the modern understanding of that task does not read it at least with sympathy, even if not fully sharing the Rilkean worldview of idealization? Only Tibetan monks and Native American elders create their art of happily scatterable sand. For the rest, the sand is a sharp and alien intrusion that needs to be answered by layered, surrounding, lasting inpourings of pearl.

Transience is only one of the possible goads into poetry. The irritant beginning might be found in the despair or spiritual ardor of Hopkins or in the desire that shook Sappho's being as wind shakes an oak. It might be Rukeyser's or Whitman's rage on behalf of those oppressed by power; it might be finding oneself, as did Celan or Hikmet or Ahkmatova or Ovid, far inside the hands of that oppression. It might be metaphysical disarray, theological puzzlement, scientific awe. It might be what Bertrand Russell described as "a temperamental unhappiness so great that but for the joy the artist derives from his work he would be driven to suicide." Rarely, it can be an excess of joy itself, an upwelling pleasure demanding expression's liberation. In whatever realm the artist's discomfort arises, it tears open the fabric of psyche and universe, leaving a hole the creative impulse rushes then to repair. The artist cannot help this any more than could a spider whose web has been shredded; his or her very survival feels at stake.

This cycle of destruction and repair is not only the writer's despair and salvation but also his or her dearest wish. As Yeats describes it in "Crazy Jane Talks with the Bishop":

"Nothing can be sole or whole that has not been rent." To participate in the creative renewal of the world is as close as we may come to touching the cloth of existence's original daybreak—in that moment, the artist is neither human nor god, neither perishable nor lasting, neither good nor bad. In that moment, when language has come awake, taken its seat in the full light of morning, and begun the tentative, much-crossed-out exploration or sure-tongued outpour, the artist is not even himself, herself. The artist and language and the page are given over to one thing alone—or rather, into no separable thing at all: they have surrendered the condition of noun to become fully verb. They are *working*. And this working, the creative act of a whole and undivided being, is the one true appetite of the writer's tongue and mind and heart, with us as long as the trout swims in the streambed while above it, slightly shadowing the surface, floats the faintest, curious glimmer of a watching human face.

River Trout

CHAPTER THREE

Seeing Through Words:
An Introduction to Bashō, Haiku,
and the Suppleness of Image

In this mortal frame of mine, which is made of a hundred bones and nine orifices, there is something, and this something is called a wind-swept spirit, for lack of a better name, for it is much like a thin drapery that is torn and swept away at the slightest stir of the wind. This something in me took to writing poetry years ago, merely to amuse itself at first, but finally making it its lifelong business. It must be admitted, however, that there were times when it sank into such dejection that it was almost ready to drop its pursuit, or again times when it was so puffed up with pride that it exulted in vain victories over others. Indeed, ever since it began to write poetry, it has never found peace with itself, always wavering between doubts of one kind and another. At one time it wanted to gain security by entering the service of a court, and at another it wished to measure the depth of its ignorance by trying to be a scholar, but it was prevented from either because of its unquenchable love of poetry. The fact is, it knows no other art than the art of writing poetry, and therefore, it hangs on to it more or less blindly.

> —Matsuo Bashō, *Journal of a Travel-Worn Satchel*
> *tr. by Nobuyuki Yuasa*

Matsuo Bashō wrote these sentences in 1687. He was forty-three. By then, his restless "wind-swept spirit" had substantially remade the shape of Japanese literature, by taking a verse form of almost unfathomable brevity and transforming it into a near-weightless, durable instrument for exploring a single moment's precise perception and resinous depths.

A few of the most well-known glimpses:

old pond:
frog leaps in
the sound of water

> furu ike ya kawazu tobikomu mizu no oto

silence:
the cicada's cry
soaks into stone

> shizukasa ya iwa ni shimiiru semi no koe

spring leaving—
birds cry,
fishes' eyes fill with tears

> yuku haru ya tori naki uo no me wa namida

horsefly
among the blossoms—
don't eat it, friend sparrow

> hana ni asobu abu na kurai so tomosuzume

in the fishmarket
even the gums of the salted sea-bream
look cold

> shiodai no haguki mo samushi uo no tana

summer grasses:
what's left
*of warriors' dreams**

> natsu gusa ya tsuwa mono domo ga yume no ato

In his poems and in his teaching of other poets, Bashō set forth a simple, deeply useful reminder: that if you see for yourself, hear for yourself, and enter deeply enough this seeing and hearing, all things will speak with and through you. "To learn about the pine tree," he told his students, "go to the pine tree; to learn from the bamboo, study bamboo." He found in every life and object an equal potential for insight and expansion. A good subject for haiku, he suggested, is a crow picking mud snails from between a rice paddy's plants. Seen truly, he taught, all things are poetic, and there's nothing that does not become a flower or moon. "But unless things are

---

*All translations not otherwise attributed are by Jane Hirshfield and Mariko Aratani.

seen with fresh eyes," he added, "nothing's worth writing down."

A wanderer all his life, both in body and spirit, Bashō concerned himself less with destination than with the quality of the traveler's attention. A poem, he said, exists only while it's on the writing desk; by the time its ink has dried, it should be recognized as just a scrap of paper. In poetry as in life, he saw each moment as gate-latch. Permeability mattered more in this process than did product or will: "If we were to gain mastery over things, we would find their lives would vanish under us without a trace."

·

The haiku form Bashō wrote in is now long familiar to Western readers: an image-based poem of seventeen sound units, written in lines of five, seven, and again five units each. (The Japanese *on* corresponds only approximately to our English syllable, though that word is generally used to translate it. In a similar vein, Japanese poetic "lines" are heard rather than written with visually separate line breaks on the page, yet most English haiku translations are set, as here, into three-line form.) One further detail is widely known in the West: the poem must evoke a particular season, by name or association. Haiku is a welcoming form, taught often in elementary school classes. In a testament to both the limitlessness of any subject and the ingenuity of haiku mind, more than nineteen thousand posted haiku about Spam—"Spamku"—can be found in an early online archive. Yet to write or read with only this understanding of the form is to go back to what haiku was before Bashō transformed it: "playful verse" is the word's literal meaning. Bashō sought more: to make of this brief, buoyant verse form a tool for emotional, psychological, and spiritual discovery, for crafting new experience as moving, expansive, and complex of ground as he felt existed in the work of earlier poets. He wanted to renovate human vision by putting what he saw into a bare handful of mostly ordinary words, and he wanted to renovate language by what he asked it to see.

Aging announced by the sensitivity of failing teeth; a street entertainer's monkey; natural-world phenomena; subtle examinations of mind and feelings—each is conveyed in Bashō's haiku by what seems a single motion of the ink brush:

growing old:
eating seaweed,
teeth hitting sand

> otoroi ya ha ni kui ateshi nori no suna

first winter downpour:
the street monkey, too,
seems to look for his small straw raincoat

> hatsu shigure saru mo ko mino o hoshi ge nari

seas darkening,
the wild duck's calls
grow faintly white

> umi kure te kamo no koe honoka ni shiroshi

the crescent moon:
it also resembles
nothing

> nani goto no mitate ni mo ni zu mika no tsuki

even in Kyoto,
hearing a cuckoo,
I long for Kyoto

> kyō nite mo kyō natsukashi ya hototogisu

Bashō's haiku, taken as a whole, conduct an extended investigation into how much can be said and known by image. When the space between poet and object disappears, Bashō taught, the object itself can begin to be fully perceived. Through this transparent seeing, our own existence is made larger. "Plants, stones, utensils, each thing has its individual feelings, similar to those of men," Bashō wrote. The statement foreshadows by three centuries T. S. Eliot's theory of the objective correlative: that the description of particular objects will evoke in us corresponding emotions.

The imagist aesthetic introduced to Western poetry near the start of the twentieth century by Ezra Pound, Amy Lowell, William Carlos Williams, and Eliot is so deeply part of current poetics that few recognize its historical origins in Asia. Haiku in its strict form has continued to draw many American contemporary writers as well, from the poet Richard Wilbur to the novelist Richard Wright, who became a master of haiku during the final years of his life, writing thousands. One abiding magnet is the paradox of haiku's scale and speed. In the moment of haiku perception, something outer is seen, heard, tasted, felt, emplaced in a scene or context. That new perception then seeds an inner response, or multiple possible responses, beyond paraphrase, name, or any other form of containment.

Here is one such poem, seated in objective perception:

> *dusk: the temple bell quiets,*
> *fragrance rings*
> *night-struck from flowers*
>
>   kane kiete hana no ka wa tsuku yūbe kana

This poem lives almost entirely in the ears and the nose, in perception both outward and accurate—the scent of certain blossoming trees does strengthen at nightfall, and orange trees (strongly night-scented) surround the temple at Ueno, where the haiku was written. The words show Bashō's characteristic synesthesia: bell-sound and twilight, flower-scent and time, are painted together into the mind, placed into a relationship that seems neither simply sequential nor logically causative. The bell of the temple stops ringing, its evening time-call over. The scent of blossoms rises into the nostrils. Inside Bashō's words, juxtaposition turns into transformation: what begins as one thing passes into another. This haiku's emotion cannot be defined except by repeating its own words; its center of gravity lies in the phenomenal world, outside the self. Yet it carries the scent and knock of strong feeling.

Haiku perception can travel the other direction as well. A thought, emotion, or circumstance already present in the mind can be chilled, heated, or soaked through by its placement into outer landscape, object, or sound. Here is a late poem whose headnote—written by Bashō—defines its image as unequivocally subjective:

"Describing what I feel"

this road
through autumn nightfall—
no one walks it

                    kono michi o yuku hito nashi ni aki no kure

The haiku describes the poet's inner state—yet without the explanatory headnote, its words appear no less external than those of the previous poem. How then should it be understood?

To read a haiku is to become its coauthor, to place yourself inside its words until they reveal one of the Proteus-shapes of your own life. The resulting experience may well differ widely between readers: image is supple, and haiku's image-based language invites an almost limitless freedom of interpretation. Written near the end of Bashō's life, "this road" can be read as a poem painting the landscape of loneliness or as a poem looking toward an unnavigable death. It can also be read as direct and immediate self-portrait: the uninhabited autumn evening and empty road may themselves *be* the poet and what he feels. Understood in this last way, the haiku presents its author as a person outside any sense of the personal self. He has fallen into a world in which there is no walker, only path.

Paths mattered to Bashō, who could—like Wordsworth or John Muir—cover twenty or thirty miles a day on foot. In his youth, it seems, he traveled only as circumstances required. In midlife, he traveled by choice, following the example of earlier poet-wanderers he admired. By the end of his life, his journeying gives off the scent of an unrefusable restlessness, a simple incapacity to stay long at home. In the opening words of *Narrow Road to the Deep North,* a prose and haiku journal describing a trip of roughly 1,500 miles undertaken by foot, boat, and horseback at the age of forty-five, Bashō wrote, "The moon and sun are travelers of a hundred generations. The years, coming and going, are wanderers too. Spending a lifetime adrift on boat decks, greeting old age while holding a horse by the mouth—for such a person, each day is a journey, and the journey itself becomes home."

Bashō's first home was Ueno, a castle town thirty miles southeast of Kyoto. Born there in 1644, and called Kinsaku as a boy, his samurai name was Matsuo Munefusa. He used at least two other pen names (Tōsei, "Green Peach," was a good choice for a not-quite-ripened poet) before taking the one by which he's now known. His father, Matsuo Yozaemon, was a low-ranking samurai who earned his living by farming and died in 1656, when Bashō was twelve.

Accounts of Bashō's life differ widely in their details. Probably a second son with four sisters, Bashō left home to work in the household of the local samurai lord and grew close to the samurai's son, Tōdō Yoshitada, two years his elder. When Bashō was twenty, both young men had work chosen for publication in an anthology of local poets. (Printing technology had recently arrived in Japan, and collections of verse were the first truly popular books.) Each also contributed to a published linked-verse *renga*— a form of poetry written by more than one person that Bashō would practice throughout his life.

The traditional form of Japanese poetry for a thousand years had been the five-line *tanka* (also called *waka*), written in the syllable count of 5–7–5–7–7. The shorter haiku form emerged from two variations of that long-standing pattern. In one, a person would write the 5–7–5 syllable opening for a tanka and another then would "cap" it by writing the closing lines. (This was both a literary game and an adaptation of the "capping verses" of Zen, written to express and demonstrate spiritual understanding.) The second, more widely practiced variation was the writing of renga—"linked verse." A renga consists of a series of three- and two-line stanzas, continuing for 36, 50, or 100 verses, in which each stanza both completes and initiates a five-line tanka when the new stanza is joined to the one that precedes or follows. Various themes and alterations of mood occur at specified points in the chain. Linked verse could be written by two people but more often was composed by a larger group of three to seven poets over the course of several hours, during which a good amount of sake or rice wine might be consumed.

The "master" poet in a renga gathering would often write the opening verse, known as the *hokku,* or "presenting verse." These hokku eventually evolved into the three-line haiku. Still, the distinctions between the forms and genres of Japanese poetry were fluid. Freestanding hokku had been written for two hundred years before Bashō's time, and among what we think of as Bashō's best-known haiku, many began as the opening verses of renga, while others were sent in letters, written in literary travel journals mixing poetry and prose, or set down within *haibun,* brief prose pieces ending in one or two poems.

To understand Bashō's place in Japanese poetry, it's useful to have some sense of the literary culture he entered. The practice of the fine arts had been central to Japanese life from at least the seventh century, and virtually all educated people painted, played musical instruments, and wrote poems. In seventeenth-century Japan, linked-verse writing was as widespread and popular as card games or Scrabble in mid-twentieth-century America. As a certain amount of alcohol was often involved, another useful comparison might be made to playing pool or darts at a local bar. The closest analogy, though, can be found in certain areas of online life today. As with the early collaborative game Dungeons and Dragons, Worlds of Warcraft, or Second Life, linked verse brought its practitioners into an interactive community that was continually and rapidly evolving. Hovering somewhere between art form and competition, renga writing provided both a party and a playing field in which intelligence, knowledge, and ingenuity might be put to the test. Add to this mix some of street rap's boundary-pushing language, Twitter's strict character count, and, finally, the video images of YouTube. Now imagine the possibility that a distinctive "high art" form of very brief films might emerge from YouTube, primarily because of one extraordinarily talented young filmmaker's creations and influence. In the realm of seventeenth-century Japanese haiku, that person was Bashō.

When Bashō was twenty-two, Yoshitada, his boyhood friend, supporter, and possibly lover, died. This loss, ten years after the death of his father, resulted once again in a kind of chrysalis-expulsion. Some accounts say Bashō entered a monastery immediately after his friend's death; others report that he fathered a child. Based on the poet's own later comments, he seems to have passed through something akin to what the Amish refer to as "wilding," a period of sampling everything the sensual world has to offer. He continued to write—his poems appear in anthologies from this time—but nothing further is known of the next five or six years. When Bashō's life comes again into view, he is living in Kyoto and the editor of a just-published volume of haiku, *The Seashell Game,* in which thirty sets of paired haiku are compared. The assembler of such a collection acted as teacher, critic, and judge, pointing out the merits and lapses of each haiku, and selecting a winner from each pair. Bashō entered two haiku of his own in the competition. Of one of his own contributions—a poem mentioning a kind of Japanese jacket—Bashō, as judge, wrote this: "Ill-tailored and badly dyed, its failures are due to lack of craftsmanship on the poet's part." The haiku lost its match to the other contestant.

At twenty-eight, Bashō moved two hundred miles to the new city of Edo (now known as Tokyo). A merchant city far from the imperial capital and its entrenched traditions, Edo attracted many young men for the social mobility, cultural upheaval, and freedom it offered; with relatively few master poets as yet in residence, Bashō's chances of finding paying students were probably higher there as well. On his departure from Kyoto, he sent a haiku to a friend in Ueno, a promise that he would return:

clouds come between friends
only briefly—
a wild goose's migration

> kumo to hedatsu tomo ka ya kari no ikiwakare

While establishing himself as a poet, Bashō worked in the offices of a city water distribution company. He also began looking after a young nephew, Tōin, who came from Ueno to live with him. Many of Bashō's students were samurai or rich merchants, and Bashō's own family origins meant he could have chosen for himself a position of greater prominence and power. All his life he remained aware of the path not taken. But poverty, for Bashō, was neither accidental nor incidental. It was a honing stone for the sharpening of awareness.

Exposed early to uncertainty, loss, and disruption, Bashō was, evidence suggests, susceptible to depression. Rather than distract himself from hardship, however, he turned toward its investigation. In his early thirties, Bashō began a period of intensive study of Zen at the temple of a local priest, Butchō. For a time he considered becoming a priest himself. Instead, at thirty-five, he took the vows of a layperson, committing to a Buddhist practice undertaken within the context and circumstances of ordinary life. During these years he also studied Taoism and the classical-era poetry of both China and Japan. He drew from and carried these works with him the remainder of his life.

Zen is less the study of doctrine than a set of tools for discovering what can be known when the world is looked at with open eyes. Poetry can be thought of in much the same way, and the recognition of impermanence, ceaseless alteration, and interdependence—the connection of each person, creature, event, and object with every other—need not be "Buddhist." These elements permeate the poetry of every tradition, from the *carpe diem* poetry of Horace and the Nahuatl "flower songs" of sixteenth-century Meso-america to the work of current American poets informed by ecology, postmodern philosophy, and quantum physics.

Still, Bashō chose Zen as the model for his life as well as for his poems, making it his path in both figurative and literal senses. Emulating both the wandering monks of his own time and the earlier Japanese Buddhist poets Saigyō and Sōgi, he began traveling for months at a time in tonsure and monk's robes, depending for his sustenance on what might be offered him along the way. "I look like a priest," he wrote in his first travel journal, "but I am a layman. I am a layman, but my head is still shaved." A sharp Zen spirit glints from his poems, in their compassion, insights, and humor, and in their quietly Buddhist stance of poet and object as "not one, not two." In one recorded dialogue with a student, Bashō instructed, "The problem with most poems is that they are either subjective or objective." "Don't you mean too subjective or too objective?" his student asked. Bashō answered, simply, "No."

The fidelity of Zen is to this world and its moment-by-moment expression of things as they are. Bashō's haiku—there are more than a thousand—have a similar allegiance. They find the gate to Zen's experience of *thusness* in the mumps-swollen cheeks of a man walking in bitter winter wind, in the sight of a woman tearing salted codfish into strips while shaded by a bucket of branches of flowering azalea. A rare haiku explicitly using the vocabulary of Zen appears in a letter Bashō sent to one of his students. He first quotes, in a headnote, a Zen master's warning: "Superficial understanding of the teachings can cause great harm." The poem following this comment reads:

how admirable—
a man who sees lightning
and not satori

inazuma ni satoranu hito no tattosa yo

Satori is the Zen term for an experience of sudden awakening into enlightenment. The image of lightning is frequently used to convey this concept. Bashō here proposes, concisely and accurately, that the truly awake person is the one who sees things simply for what they themselves are. Any idea-awareness is already a separation and stepping away.

Shinto, Japan's other major spiritual tradition, saturates Bashō's poems as well, most noticeably in the importance given to place and the way that particular places come to embody certain feelings and themes. Shinto's *kami* spirits live not in generality, abstraction, or paradise but embedded in the earthly, visitable, and local—shrines, mountains, islands, fields, and trees. Bashō's lifelong practice of poetry pilgrimage joined Zen non-attachment with Shinto's deep-seated spirit of place.

•

Of the haiku Bashō wrote during his late twenties and early thirties, the earliest were often clever or charming, though even these poems often reflect the poet's innate compassion and deep sympathy for all beings. Some clearly respond to the circumstances of his personal life. Many show an increasing involvement with Chinese poetry, Zen, and the growing desire to find in a single moment, fully perceived, the multifaceted depths we feel also in Cezanne's painted apples or Dürer's hare inked into place amid grasses.

Here are a few of these early poems. The first was written at age twenty-two, when Bashō was attempting the cleverness then popular among cutting-edge poets:

looking exactly like
blue flag iris: blue flag iris
inside the water's shadow

        kakitsubata nitari ya nitari mizu no kage

The main point in the original Japanese is the poem's mirroring construction: two identical words at the haiku's center replicate both visually and in sound what is being described. In Japanese, which is written vertically, the visual onomatopoeia is even clearer: a small "cutting-word," *ya,* creates the slim line of water dividing the flower stem's two apparently equal selves. Yet even in this poem of displayed wit, we find also the echo of a Buddhist question addressed through centuries of Japanese poetry: What in life is real, what is illusion?

In other early poems, Bashō's distinctive perception, empathy, humor, and friendship with all existence begin to emerge:

"Written at the house of a person whose child has died"

a withered, leaning, out-of-joint world—
bamboo
upside down under snow

        shiore fusu ya yo wa sakasama no yuki no take

a cuckoo!
masters of haiku
vanish

        hototogisu ima wa haikaishi naki yo kana

shy
above flowers' faces,
a hazy moon

        hana no kao ni hareute shite ya oborozuki

a hangover?
who cares,
while there are blossoms

        futsukayoi mono kawa hana no aru aida

cutting a tree,
seeing the sawn trunk it grew from:
tonight's moon

        ki o kirite motokuchi miru ya kyōno tsuki

This tree-cutting haiku presents fertile ground for looking more deeply at poetic image, both in haiku and in general.

In Japanese poetry, allusion to the moon refers, first, always, to the moon itself, clear or cloud-scuffed in the night sky. But the image holds, almost always, some additional meaning—not infrequently, a Buddhist reference to awakened understanding. With this in mind, various readings of "cutting a tree" begin to emerge. It can be understood as a glimpse of enlightenment—an opening of consciousness in this case precipitated by the ordinary act of felling a tree. It can be read as bitter: the moon is as opaque to the mind as a tree stump. It can be read as comic: the poet, having had no time to look up, finds the moon right under his eyes. It can be read as luminously descriptive: the yellow color of a rising moon recognized as exactly the color of fresh-cut pine. It can be taken as describing the experience that came from sawing down a tree, as describing the moon, or as offering a small Buddhist parable about long effort leading to sudden awakening. It may be that Bashō intended all these meanings. Equally, it could be that he had no intention in mind at all, and the juxtaposition of moon and tree trunk simply arose, amid the scent of fresh sawdust.

Haiku's suggestiveness is penumbra, not umbrella. Still,

human vision is subjective, and there is a further complication for Western readers: the haiku read alone on a
page, blurred by lack of shared cultural reference and by
translation, was often originally written in circumstances
both specific and knowable by its original readers. As
mentioned earlier, many of Bashō's haiku were composed
as part of linked-verse gatherings. Others were written
for poetry competitions with assigned subjects. Many
were personal communications—messages sent between
friends, between guest and host or teacher and student—
or placed within travel journals or the extended prose set-
tings of haibun, which gave them added meaning. Some
were written about paintings, places, objects, or played on
then-well-known phrases now opaque to even contemporary Japanese readers. Art can be defined as beauty able to
transcend the circumstances of its making. Still, if a person finds a particular haiku baffling or lifeless, that may be
because some essential piece of information is missing. A
hangover is universally comprehensible. That the specialized lumbering term translated here as "sawn [tree] trunk"
is a word that can also mean "source," in an ontological and
metaphysical sense, is not—though, once this is pointed
out, the implication is clearly resident in the originating
image.

·

At the time he began to take writing poetry seriously,
Bashō was influenced by the rapidly changing aesthetics
and schools of poetry around him. It was a period as volatile as that in American poetry between the early 1950s,

when most poets worked in formal meter and rhyme, and the late 1970s, when some poets turned to using language in ways similar to the abstract expressionists' use of paint. Between these aesthetic periods come the revolutions made by the Beat poets, the radically confessional poetry of Lowell and Plath, and the "deep image" poetry of Robert Bly, James Wright, and others.

These aesthetic transformations parallel—oddly, but closely—those of Bashō's own lifetime. In each case, a sudden loosening of language, taste, and subject matter breaks open arthritic conventions of poetic decorum and is then followed by the turn toward a poetry quieter of surface and more inwardly centered. Bashō's first haiku were written under the influence of a school that advocated wordplay, transgression, and turns on well-known earlier classical works. He next wrote poems of simpler, everyday language and imagery that used humor and earthiness as a way to break poetry's diction free from old ruts. (One haiku from this time parodies a classical scene of courtly love by showing a female cat in heat scrambling over a broken-down cookstove to reach her tomcat lover.) These taboo-breaking intentions were not Bashō's invention; they were the fashion of the day. Still, this early foundation in an aggressively transgressive style instilled in Bashō the confidence that poetry was a medium in which almost anything could be said. "Madman's poetry" one such school was called. Bashō kept this grant of liberation throughout his life, turning it toward continually deepening ends until its final appearance in his late-life advocacy of the haiku of "lightness."

The practice of Zen also works to free the mind from its habits of conventional perception. By 1678, Bashō no longer studied with others. Now a teacher himself, he began developing his own sense of haiku's possibilities, intentions, and role. For inspiration, he turned less to his contemporaries than to ancient Japanese and Chinese poems reflecting Buddhist and Taoist themes, especially the works of Sōgi, Saigyō, and the Chinese poets Tu Fu and Li Po—poetic tunings that, three centuries later, would come to influence the deep-image poets of America as well.

In 1680, two events, one inward, the other outer, can be taken as markers for the fruition of Bashō's efforts. The inner boundary marker can be found in a haiku often referred to as Bashō's first mature work:

on a leafless branch,
a crow's settling:
autumn nightfall

> kareeda ni karasu no tomarikeri aki no kure

When autumn's diminishments and an ordinary crow are felt to be beauty as much as loss, loss is unpinned from its usual meanings. In Japanese, the alloy of beauty and sadness found in this poem is described as *sabi*—a quality at the heart of much of Bashō's mature writing. The noun *sabishi* is generally translated as "loneliness," or sometimes "solitude," but the word originates in associations very close to those found in this haiku: it holds the feeling of whatever is chill, withered, and pared down to the leanness of essence. "The works of other schools of poetry are like colored paintings; my disciples paint with black ink," Bashō later said. To feel *sabi* is to feel keenly one's own sharp and particular existence amid its own impermanence, and to value the singular moment as William Blake did "infinity in the palm of your hand"—to feel it to be as precise and almost weightless as a sand grain, yet also vast. In making the expression of *sabi* one of haiku's goals, Bashō turned his own and his students' writing toward a new spirit. The gravitational pull of that renewed seriousness shifted haiku writing from the construction of entertainment to the making of art.

Haiku's imagery is not confined to the lyrical, as we've already seen. "Eat vegetable soup, not duck stew," Bashō told his students, calling plainness and oddity the bones of haiku. Another poem from this time begins with a headnote:

"The rich enjoy the finest meats and ambitious young men save money by eating root vegetables. I myself am simply poor."

snowy morning—
alone,
still able to chew dried salmon

                yuki no ashita hitori karazake wo kami etari

In seventeenth-century Japan, *karazake* was commoner's food. For Bashō, to speak of eating dried salmon on a cold morning was neither complaint nor self-pity—it was an evocation of *wabi.* A concept often linked to *sabi,* and equally important to Bashō's work, *wabi* conveys the beauty of the most ordinary circumstances and objects. A farmer's worn hemp jacket, a plain fired-clay cup, the steam rising from a boiling teapot—these are wabi's essence. A gold-and-cloisonné bowl or ornate silk clothes are its opposite. In the spirit of wabi, then, this poem mulls the deep satisfaction of a life stripped almost bare.

Of the two transition markers that signal Bashō's maturing as person and poet, the inward change was his embodiment of a Zen spirit, *wabi-sabi,* and plainness. The outer change was an alteration of circumstance that led to the name by which he's now known. In feudal-era Japan, "town teachers," as they were called, lived by the support of students and wealthy patrons. Gifts might be monetary, but as often took the form of rice, books, sandals, and clothes. For nine years in Edo, Bashō had lived in rented housing, on a combination of salary from his water-company work, fees for correcting poems, and teaching donations. In the winter of 1680, shortly after Bashō wrote his haiku on the autumn crow, one of his followers built him a simple thatch-roofed hut on the bank of the Sumida River in Fukugawa, a quiet outskirt of the city. That spring, another student planted a kind of Japanese plantain or banana tree in its front garden—a plant known in Japanese as a *bashō.* The house came to be called the Bashō Hut, and its inhabitant soon took the name as well.

Many years later, when living in a different hut near the site of his first one, Bashō wrote two different versions of a haibun on the occasion of transplanting some shoots from his old bashō tree to a new location in his garden. Here is an excerpt, ending with its haiku:

What year did I come to nest in this area, planting a single bashō tree? The climate here must be good for it—many new trunks have grown up around the first one, their leaves so thick that they crowd my garden and shade my house-eaves. People named my hut after this plant. Every year, old friends and students who've grown to like my tree take cuttings or divide the roots and carry them off to replant far and wide.

One year my heart set itself on a trip to the northern interior, and I abandoned this Bashō Hut. . . . My sadness at leaving the tree was surprisingly strong. After five springs and autumns away, I've now returned, and my sleeves are wet with tears. The scent of blossoming oranges is near; my friends' warmth has not changed. There's no way I'll leave it behind again.

My new thatch-roofed cottage, near the site of the earlier one, fits me well, with its three small rooms. . . . I've transplanted five bashō saplings so that the moon, seen through their branches, will be even more beautiful and moving. The bashō's leaves are over seven feet long. When they rip almost to their center ribs in the wind, it's as painful as seeing a phoenix whose tail has been broken, as pitiful as the sight of a torn green fan.

Sometimes the bashō tree blossoms, but its flowers are small. Its thick stalk remains untouched by any axe. Like the famous ancient tree of the mountains, the bashō's useless nature is itself the reason to admire it. A monk caressed that mountain tree with his brush to learn its ways; a scholar watched its leaves unfold to inspire his studies. But I'm not like either of them. I just rest in the shade of the leaves I love because they are so easily torn.

bashō leaves
will cover its post-beams—
hut of the moon

> bashōba o hashira ni kaken io no tsuki

By the time he wrote this, the poet had long been called by the bashō tree's name, and each of the major themes of his life appears in this dense meditation on the plant whose identity merged with the poet's own—his restless wanderings and sensual awareness; his transplanter's impulse toward revision and renewal; his empathic identification with the tree's fragile leaves; the importance of friendship; the desire for unusual beauty; and the continuing examination of both inner and outer worlds undertaken by seeing through words, both those of earlier writers and his own.

The aesthetics of finding beauty in spareness and poverty should not disguise the genuine hardship of Bashō's life. His grass hut, however scenic, had neither a well nor plumbing. In one haibun written late in 1681, Bashō quotes a few lines by the Chinese poet Tu Fu and then says, "I can see the wabi here, but I don't take any joy in it. I'm superior to Tu Fu in only one thing: the frequency with which I fall sick. Hidden away behind the bashō leaves of this rickety hut, I call myself, 'Useless Old Bum.'" One of several accompanying haiku reads:

bitter ice-shards
moisten
the mud-rat's throat

> kōri nigaku enso ga nodo wo uruoseri

The haiku carries a headnote: "I buy water at this grass-roofed hut." The poem alludes to a statement from the Chinese Taoist writings of Chuang-Tzu: "A sewer rat drinks only enough from the river to quench its thirst." Bashō's container of purchased water, which froze often during long winter nights, may well have reminded him of that image. Still, this haiku seems as much a portrait of genuine bitterness as of Taoist austerity.

Another haibun from this period of Bashō's life, titled "Sleeping Alone in a Grass Hut," includes this poem:

the bashō thrashing in wind,
rain drips into an iron tub—
a listening night

> bashō nowaki shite tarai ni ame wo kiku yo kana

The haiku is a study in sounds, textures, and scale, and in exposure, both exterior and interior. The banana tree's leaves are torn by the typhoon winds—the storm was the fiercest in many years—whose huge sound passes over the poem. The sound of water falling drop by drop into a washtub (possibly outside, but more likely catching water from a roof leak) is near, precise, and intimate; yet its purchase on the attention is as large as the storm's. Bashō tree leaves tearing in wind were a long-standing image in classical Chinese and Japanese poems; dripping roofs and ordinary metal basins, less so. The balance of the minute and the vast, of the personal and forces that care nothing about the personal, of idealized, "poetic" experience and the actual living through of a major storm, is registered in each drop of water striking iron.

In January 1683, a year after Bashō moved into his Fukugawa hut, a fire swept through much of Edo. Bashō survived only by jumping into the river, using a soaked reed mat to shield his head from the heat and smoke. He was forced to move into a patron's house, far from the city. Then, that summer, his mother died. In the fall, his students found him new lodgings in a rundown house not far from his burned one and supplied him with household items, a few clothes, and a large hollow gourd to hold rice, which they regularly filled. When the New Year (early spring, in the traditional Japanese calendar) arrived, Bashō marked it with this haiku:

I'm wealthy—
going into the new year
with 20 pounds of old rice

        ware tomeri shinnen furuki kome goshō

Bashō revised his haiku, haibun, and journals throughout his life. Not infrequently the direction was toward a diminishment of ego and self, but there are also poems in which he experimented with various alternative verbs or subject lines to feel their effects. Should a poem be about "loneliness" or "stillness"? Should a sound "soak," "pierce," or "stain"? These alterations show that even his most seemingly unstudied and artless works were often produced by a method quite unlike what is sometimes described as a "Zen" "first thought, best thought." A later revision of the above poem removes the first line's self-description:

spring begins—
going into the new year
with 20 pounds of old rice
> haru tatsu ya shinnen furuki kome goshō

A few years later, another haiku seems to recall that rice-storing kitchen gourd, though here it appears to be empty:

my one-possession
world,
a lightweight gourd
> mono hitotsu waga yo wa karoki hisago kana

The words do not reveal the poet's attitude about the situation. I myself lean toward the interpretation of a liberating portability of existence: this poem was written during the time of Bashō's travels, by a man long used, by then, to many losses.

Not long after the fire that took his first hut, Bashō published the first collection holding the work of his followers. Its title, *Shriveled Chestnuts,* points toward Bashō's aesthetic of valuing the valueless; he said of the book's "shriveled chestnuts," "They may be small, but their taste is sweet." Yet along with his increasing success as a poetry master, Bashō grew, it seems, increasingly unsettled. When he received an invitation to visit some former students, he began preparing for a lengthy trip. He shaved his head, put on the robes of a mendicant monk, and in the fall of 1684 set out with a friend on a seven-month-long journey by foot, horseback, and ferry. The trip would include a visit to his mother's grave before going on to places made famous by earlier Japanese writers. It was the first of five such trips, each recorded in a published journal mixing poems written during his travels with prose descriptions of places, people, and events.

Bashō called his account of this early trip *The Journal of a Weather-Beaten Skeleton,* and its first sentences and opening haiku set the tone:

I set out on a trip of a thousand miles without any supplies, my walking-stick the staff of an ancient said to have vanished one night under a midnight moon. As I left my run-down hut, the wind's sound over the river was odd and cold.

roadside-skeleton-thoughts:
wind penetrates
through to the heart

                    nozarashi o kokoro ni kaze no shimu mi kana

One Zen saying proposes, "Live as if you were already dead." Bashō's journal's title seems to carry that spirit. But the effect of the haiku itself is quite different. Chilled from the first moment of his departure, the poet felt cold winds going through him as if through a skeleton's exposed ribs. Travel was perilous, Bashō's health not strong, and the image of himself as that passed-by skeleton, its bones left out to weather by the road, would haunt him throughout the journey.

Another reminder of death's omnipresence appeared soon after, when Bashō saw a small child, perhaps two years old, abandoned by the road. The early 1680s were years of famine, flood, fire, social turmoil, and desperate poverty, and the sight was not uncommon. Still, for a modern reader, this incident is the most difficult to accept of any in Bashō's life: he tossed some food to the child and rode on, thinking about fate, finally deciding that, however sorrowful, the child's abandonment was "heaven's will." The haiku he wrote afterward, though, is an undisguised rebuke—to society, to poetry, to fate, and to the writer himself:

the cries of monkeys
are hard for a person to bear—
what of this child, given to autumn winds?
> saru wo kiku hito sutego ni aki no kaze ikani

Shortly afterward in the journal, the theme of impermanence appears yet again, though in a different mood:

the roadside blooming
mallow:
eaten by my horse
> michinobe no mukuge wa uma ni kuwarekeri

These three haiku, placed near one another at the start of Bashō's journey, have the effect of reminding the reader, and perhaps the poet, that all things vanish, sometimes tragically, sometimes ridiculously. When he reached Ueno, his brother showed him a lock of their late mother's white hair. The haiku he wrote in response:

if I took it into my hand,
would hot tears make it vanish?
autumn frost
>   te ni toraba kien namida zo atsuki oki no shimo

Leaving Edo required crossing a high mountain pass. Famous for its view of Fuji, it was the vantage point of many well-known poems. Here is Bashō's contribution:

mist, rain,
not seeing Fuji—
an interesting day!
>   kirishigure Fuji wo minu hi zo omoshiroki

The haiku's response reflects the spirit of Bashō's early teachers, who suggested that haiku's essence was to find, in the face of the long-familiar, something not yet said. The poem might almost be translated, "Mist, rain, not seeing Fuji—what luck!"

·

During the ten years of journeys that filled his forties, Bashō stopped to record his responses to temples and shrines, the sites of historical battles, ruined huts where earlier Buddhist poets had lived. He met and separated from friends, shared his sleeping quarters with fleas, prostitutes, and pissing horses, and his robes with lice. He participated in linked-verse gatherings, returned home and repeatedly set out again, published haiku, renga, and the five major journals describing his travels. Various haibun describe briefer trips to places famous for moon viewing and also retreats undertaken in two borrowed houses, "The Unreal Hut," on Lake Biwa, and "The Villa of Fallen Persimmons," near Kyoto. The best known of all Bashō's journeys is the 1,500-mile expedition recorded in the journal *Narrow Road to the Far North*. The title is sometimes rendered as "Narrow Roads to the Deep Interior"—the word *oku* carries both geographical and metaphorical meanings (as it does in English, when we refer, for instance, to the "interior" of both Alaska and the self).

Bashō's traveling was an exercise in response and immersion, an extended practice of image and statement. Each day in a new place brought changed circumstance and the possibility of a new subject, particularly for a poet seeking to bring into Japanese poetry ordinary objects and activities previously ignored. While visiting a temple—and perhaps assisting in the kitchen, since kitchen practice marks both good Zen and good guests—Bashō wrote:

coldness—
deep-rooted leeks
washed white

                nebuka shiroku araiagetaru samusa kana

Any cook knows that cleaning the soil from leeks requires much time, and the coldness here is in the leeks, in the icy winter stream water they were washed in, and in the poet's and reader's own hands, all at once. Even the leeks' whiteness enters the body: chilled hands grow pale.

This transparency of boundary is one of haiku's most basic devices and instructions, and the permeability of self to non-self is made explicit in another poem from this period. At a river crossing, Bashō's host treated the traveler with kindness, then asked for a written memento of the now-famous poet's visit. Bashō wrote:

> *in rented rooms*
> *signing my name:*
> *"cold winter rains"*

> yado karite na o nanora suru shigure kana

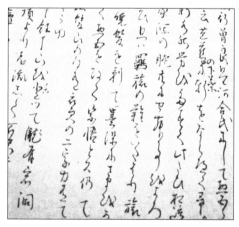

Calligraphy by Bashō

Renown came to Bashō as a teacher as well as a poet during these final ten years of his life. The increasing support for his ideas and poems must have gratified; yet the ensuing demands also distracted and at times, it seems, clearly annoyed. To one aspiring student, he sent some sharp words counseling independence, along with this haiku:

don't copy me,
like the second half
of a cut melon!

    ware ni niru na futatsu ni wareshi makuwauri

At other times, Bashō reminded his disciples of the words of the ninth-century Buddhist teacher and poet Kukai: "Do not follow the ancient masters, seek what they sought." However strong his opinions and theories, Bashō's primary allegiance was to the living moment and its accurate, full-hearted presentation. Of the formal requirements of haiku, he said, "If you have three or four, even five or seven extra syllables but the poem still sounds good, don't worry about it. But if one syllable stops the tongue, look at it hard."

·

As he turned fifty, Bashō, living in what was now his third Bashō Hut, famously closed his brushwood gate. At the year's start, he wrote in a letter, "Crushed by other people and their needs, I can find no calmness of mind." He was caring for his ill nephew Tōin, who now had a family, having married a former nun, Jutei, and fathered three children.

Students and fellow poets dropped by to ask for advice, exchange poems, and talk; invitations to poetry gatherings were ceaseless. In April, Tōin died. In mid-August, Bashō shut himself off from all visitors, resolving to find a way to free himself from outward obligation and its accompanying exhaustion and resentment. Two months later, he cut through the morning-glory vine overgrowing his hut's entrance and emerged with a new philosophy, in life and in haiku. He called it *karumi*: "lightness."

Bashō's transformation of spirit can be seen by comparing two haiku. The first—preceding Bashō's retreat into seclusion—was written on New Year's Day, 1693:

> *year after year,*
> *the monkey's face*
> *wears a monkey's mask*
>
>> toshidoshi ya saru ni kisetaru saru no men

The second was written the last day of that year:

> *year-end-thought:*
> *one night,*
> *even a thief came to visit*
>
>> nusubito no ōta yo mo ari toshi no kure

The earlier, New Year's Day haiku is a portrait of entrapment within the social. Beneath persona, it says, there is only more persona—a street entertainer's monkey doing the same tricks over and over, or a man (as Bashō commented while talking with a student about this poem) making the same mistakes repeatedly, in an unchanging life. The second haiku, written a year later, surely refers as well to the overly social life Bashō had been leading, but here, bitterness has vanished, and the poet seems less rueful than amused. This haiku evokes the famous story of a Chinese hermit who, finding that his hut has been robbed, goes running after the thief with a left-behind, heavy pot in his hand: "Thief, stop! You forgot this!"

A few more poems from this time:

New Year's Eve cleaning—
the carpenter hangs a shelf
in his own house

> susu haki wa ono ga tana tsuru daiku kana

spring rain—
roof leak drizzling
through a hanging wasps' nest

> harusame ya hachi no su tsutao yane no mori

cool, cool:
noon-napping,
feet on a wall

> hiya hiya to kabe wo fumaete hirune kana

morning glory:
a day-flowering lock
bolts my gate

> asagao ya hiru wa jō orosu mon no kaki

in morning dew
smudged, cool,
a muddy melon

asatsuyu ni yogore te suzushi uri no tsuchi

lightning—
a night heron's cry
flies into darkness

inazuma ya yami no kata yuku goi no koe

•

In February 1694, Bashō wrote a friend that he felt his end was near, but he nonetheless made plans for another journey. Illness prevented his leaving until June, and even then he was able to travel only because he was accompanied by one of Tōin and Jutei's sons and by Sora, an old road companion and friend. Carried by litter, he arrived at Ueno too weak to see visitors or to teach. While he was there, Jutei died, and he sent her son home. He and Sora continued on to both the Unreal Hut and the Villa of Fallen Persimmons, places of refuge familiar from earlier trips. In late August, Bashō returned to his family home, where his students built him a small grass hut behind his brother's. This visit, he was stronger. He continued attempting to communicate his new ideas to students, who he worried were not comprehending well his encouragement to see and write "the way a clear, shallow river runs over a sandy bed." In October he went on to Osaka, continuing to teach and participate in renga gatherings despite headaches, fever, and chills.

The haiku from the time of these travels show Bashō fully aware of the seriousness of his condition. Yet they maintain his renewed aesthetic of transparence and lightness:

this autumn,
why do I grow old?
a bird entering clouds

> kono aki wa nande toshi yoru kumo ni tori

white chrysanthemum:
not one speck of dust
meets the eye

> shiragiku no me ni tate te miru chiri mo nashi

clear moon,
a boy afraid of foxes
walked home by his lover

> tsuki sumu ya kitsune kowagaru chigo no tomo

deep autumn—
my neighbor,
what is he doing?

> aki fukaki tonari wa nani wo suru hito zo

Bashō spoke of the need to turn his thoughts from the life of this world to Buddhist teachings, but he said he could not—poems continued to come. His final haiku was written November 25, 1694, a few days before his death:

on a journey, ill,
dreams scouring on
through exhausted fields

> tabi ni yande yume wa kareno wo kake meguru

Having written it, he immediately composed another poem describing the wanderings of his dreaming mind, and called in Shikō, one of his students, asking which he preferred. Shikō failed to catch the first line and, too embarrassed to ask, simply said he thought the earlier one unsurpassable. Bashō answered, "I know I shouldn't be writing haiku now, so close to my death. But poetry is all I've thought of for over fifty years. When I sleep, I dream about hurrying down a road under morning clouds or evening mist. When I awaken I'm captivated by the mountain stream's interesting sounds or the calls of wild birds. Buddha called such attachment wrong, and of this I am guilty. But I cannot forget the haiku that have filled my life."

On November 26, Bashō wrote letters, including one in which he apologized to his older brother for dying first. The next day, he asked the students who had gathered around him to compose poems, but added that he wouldn't comment on them: "You must understand, your teacher no longer exists." He mostly slept after that, but on the twenty-eighth, he woke up during a warm midday to find his students quietly trying to catch the many flies that had gathered on the room's shoji-paper walls. He laughed, and said of the flies, "They seem happy about this unexpected gift." The comment is characteristic. A few hours later, he died in his sleep.

☙

His poetry, Bashō once told a student, was like a fan in winter, a stove in summer. As with so many of his images, the statement can be taken in more than one way. It can be read as a praise of uselessness, saying that poetry, like the bashō tree, is a thing to be loved precisely because it has no utilitarian purpose—by Bashō's own account, that is what he meant. But the description can also be read as an advocacy of intensification: whatever a person's experience, bringing it into a poem will strengthen it further. In some subtle way, these two ideas are not so disconnected as they at first may seem.

What does knowledge of Bashō offer a contemporary Western reader? Foremost, the poems themselves. Bashō's haiku, once read, stay in the mind and return there at odd times, bringing their unexpected expansions to moments of heat or thirst, to aging teeth, a sudden experience of coolness in mid-August, or the first wintry rains. Next, perhaps, there is the proof they offer that even the briefest form of poetry can have a wingspan of immeasurable breadth. Bashō's seventeen-syllable haiku, looked at closely, are much like Emily Dickinson's poems. They are small but many (both poets left behind more than a thousand poems), and the work of each of these poets crosses implausibly wide, variable, and precise terrains of mind and world. Bashō's haiku describe and feel, think and debate. They test ideas against the realities of observation; they renovate, expand, and intensify both experience and the range of language.

Bashō's poems also instruct in an alternative possibility

of being. One useful way to approach a haiku is to understand each of its parts as pointing toward both world and self. Read this way, haiku remind us that a person should not become too fixed in a singular sense of what the self might consist of or know, or where it might reside.

winter day:
on horseback,
a frozen shadow

> fuyu no hi ya bajō ni kōru kagebōshi

wild seas—
sweeping over the island of exiles,
heaven's river of stars

> araumi ya Sado ni yokotau amanogawa

New Year's Eve year-forgetting party—
wondering what fish feel,
what birds feel?

> uo tori no kokoro wa shirazu toshiwasure

the cicada's singing
does not show its body
is already dying

> yagate shinu keshiki wa miezu semi no koe

too ill to eat
even a rice cake—
peach trees in flower

> wazurae ba mochi o mo kuwazu momo no hana

mountain cuckoo,
sing my grief-notes
into sabi

        uki ware wo sabishi garase yo kanko dori

sea slugs,
frozen alive:
one body

        ikinagara hitotsu ni kōru namako kana

octopus-catching jars—
the summer moon's
brief dreams

        tako tsubo ya hakanaki yume o natsu no tsuki

These haiku bow to what lies on both sides of the skin's millimeter-thick boundary. The reader who enters Bashō's perceptions fully can't help but find in them a kind of liberation. They unfasten the mind from any single or absolute story, unshackle us from the clumsy dividing of world into subjective and objective, self and other, illness and blossom, freedom and capture. Some haiku seem to be reports of internal awareness, some seem to point at the external, but Bashō's work as a whole awakens us to the necessary permeability of all to all. Awareness of the mind's movements makes clear that it is the mind's nature to move. Feeling within ourselves the lives of others (people, creatures, plants, and things) who share this world is what allows us to feel as we do at all. First comes the sight of a block of sea slugs frozen while still alive, then the sharp, kinesthetic comprehension of the inseparability of the suffering of one from the suffering of all. First comes hearing the sound of one bird singing, then the recognition that solitude can carry its own form of beauty, able to turn pain into pellucid depth.

Bashō began by writing haiku as a pastime, amusing himself as a young man by trying to make something new, unexpected, and of the moment. One of the more unexpected things he did was then to turn that idle search to serious use. In his life, as in his poems, he continually took the unconventional turn, abandoning his place in the traditional structures of class, leaving the cultural center for its periphery in both geographical and intellectual realms, choosing to live as wanderer, outsider, provincial. He consistently chose the open over the known, chose to grow old sleeping in fields on grass pillows or in lice-ridden inns. He preferred a traveler's straw hat with a few words inked inside its rim to the solidity of roofs. At the end, his model for haiku was the artless expression of a child at play.

"The invincible power of poetry," Bashō wrote, "has reduced me to the condition of a tattered beggar." The statement was literal. One haiku expresses gratitude for the gift of a new pair of straw sandals, with straps the color of blue iris, at the start of a trip, and Bashō noted that he was always quite safe from robbers, as he carried nothing of value to anyone else. Yet the statement points to another level of meaning as well: a poet's existence is necessarily open to dependence, to interdependence. Bashō's haiku are the record of what the world placed in the open begging bowl of his life and his perceptions.

The words he wrote on the rim of his homemade travel-ing hat can be translated, loosely, as these:

Under this world's long rains,
here passes
poetry's makeshift shelter.

        yo ni furu mo sarani sōgi no yadori kana

CHAPTER FOUR

Thoreau's Hound:
Poetry and the Hidden

I long ago lost a hound, a bay horse, and a turtle dove, and am still on their trail," wrote Henry David Thoreau, in *Walden*. "Many are the travelers I have spoken to concerning them, describing their tracks and what calls they answered to. I have met one or two who had heard the hound, and the tramp of the horse, and even seen the dove disappear behind a cloud, and they seemed as anxious to recover them as if they had lost them themselves."

And here is a perception quite different, yet not unrelated, from Ralph Waldo Emerson's "Experience": "Sleep lingers all our lifetime about our eyes, as night hovers all day in the boughs of the fir tree."

Homo sapiens sapiens: it is the name of a species that wants to *know*. Yet a counter-thirst exists in us as well, for something the opposite of knowledge, of too easy exposure. Who would think Emerson's fir tree more beautiful if the darkness were stripped from its depths, or prefer Thoreau's elusive turtle dove caged and in hand? "Heard melodies are sweet," wrote Keats, "but those unheard are sweeter." A fidelity to the ungraspable can be found at the root of both biological existence and what we experience as beauty; the steepest pitches of the heart and mind make their own shade. Within that cool and dimness, emotions and thoughts small as new mosses and lichens begin the slow, green colonizations of incipient life.

Concealment does not presume conscious intention. Perspective, though, is essential: literal hiddenness requires the physical presence of both a seer and something that might have been seen. The English word "hiding" is sewn from the hides of animals' bodies. Both words derive from Old German and Sanskrit terms for protection, and it's worth noticing that many animals' skins offer not only a physically protective membrane but also the visual protection of coloring, whether by strategies of camouflage or drabness. The German *huota* lingers on as well in the intimate dwelling place that is a "hut."

Hiddenness, then, is a sheltering enclosure—one we stand sometimes outside of, other times within. One of its more subtle homes is the Ryoan-ji rock garden in Kyoto: wherever in it a person stands, one of the fifteen rocks cannot be seen. The garden's positioned stones remind us there is always something unknowable and invisible beyond what can be perceived or comprehended, yet as real as any other rock amid the raked gravel. Subjectivity's perimeters, not the objective world, create the unknown.

Ryoan-ji Rock Garden

•

In Western literature, explorations of hiddenness go back to the beginning. It may be that the largest initial hiddenness and mystery is that which surrounds birth and death, and the central axis of the Sumerian *Gilgamesh,* our earliest extant epic, is the unhiding of death to human perception. To accept death's irrefusable threshold is the entrance price for full consciousness—self-awareness is needed to recognize the vanishing of selves. The joined realization of separateness, connection, and transience propels Gilgamesh's outcry upon his friend Enkidu's death, "This will happen also to me!" In that moment might lie the division between animal consciousness and the fully human—while animals may feel, may dream, may solve, it does not seem as yet that they grapple with the foreknowledge of death. Only we live face-to-face with that walled-shut gate.

Hiddenness saturates also the works of ancient Greece. The tragedies turn on the wheel-rim of an insufficient knowledge, compassion, or vision; concealment both shadows and charges the Homeric epics. The *Odyssey,* in particular, can be read as a consummate study of hiddenness in a human life, of the way it can, rightly welcomed, develop and temper our nature. An odd symmetry of disappearance marks the opening of each of Homer's epics. After the *Iliad*'s initiating quarrel, Achilles retires to his tent, not to reemerge for another eight books. For the first four books of the *Odyssey,* Odysseus is similarly unseen: he has been "banished into black obscurity" in the goddess Calypso's grottoes. During his subsequent wanderings, Odysseus is dipped repeatedly into the condition of the unseen. He is concealed in dense thorn bushes and mists; he escapes the cave of the Cyclops Polyphemus by suspending himself beneath the belly of a thick-wooled ram; when he finally reenters Ithaca, he is disguised in the rags of an aged beggar. This is not the first time. When the man of craft, as he is called, scouts the city of Troy before executing his plan for the Trojan Horse—another stratagem of invisibility, it need hardly be noted—he also dresses as a beggar, to the point of covering himself in self-inflicted bruises. Who would look for a hero in such battered form?

The Homeric poems are filled with sea storms and battles, event and drama. Yet the stories pivot upon strategic or sullen withdrawals, on the threshold moments when things are not what they seem. A king and a heroic warrior each behave like a spoiled child. A wooden horse is abandoned on a beach by a seemingly departed army. A far-traveling hero learns to trust no one, to lie about his name and history, to receive the abuse of a goatherd and keep his tongue silent. Even the goddess Athena, upon entering into human events to ensure an outcome, disguises herself in the form of a shepherd or serving girl or long-trusted friend. When the gods appear in the world of ordinary beings, they borrow the shapes of the earth.

Achilles in the cloak of his tent, Odysseus wrapped in his guise of beggar, are persons removed from their identities and signature powers. Achilles, though, emerges from his angry retreat essentially the same proud man, while Odysseus learns from the fabric of hiddenness a new power, learns that fabrication itself is a power. Over the course of his much-troubled wanderings, he grows increasingly skillful at knowing what stories to speak aloud, what facts to keep hidden, shielded by silence. The man of craft—learning to suppress his old reliance on courage and boldness, learning to govern with increasing humility his tongue and its words—is the one who escapes the tragic hero's fate, to know again family and kingdom.

The lesson runs deep in both literature and the psyche: survival depends on an intimate, attuned comfort with similitude and the art of disguise. I asked a biologist friend, Michael Dickinson, to muse on this subject. He replied:

For most of life on the planet, being hidden is the default condition. Visibility typically costs you your life, or at least a good meal. Sex or an advertisement of a poisonous disposition are the only reasons anything with a pulse and a wink of sense would want to be conspicuous. This is why we are generally disappointed when we don our Vibram soles and trek through ticks and prickly shrubs to view wildlife. Wildlife are usually annoyed at being seen, if they are seen at all. As hiddenness is the default, visibility is a luxury. Rarely are earth-colored tones the symbols of opulence and royal blood. We are most comfortable being hidden but we yearn to be seen.

The inventions of biological hiddenness are countless, witty, wily, and poignant. Insects mimic twigs and flower parts, the sexual partners or foods of their prey, whatever is poisonous to those for whom they themselves are prey. Flowers seeking fertilization take the form and scents of the sexual partners of insects. A cohort of caterpillars bands together to travel in a single column, mirroring the body of a large and dangerous snake. There are spiders that look like bird droppings, pipefish that sleep vertically to blend with surrounding reeds. Octopus and cuttlefish change the color and texture of their skins to match the surfaces over which they travel; a jellyfish hides in its own transparence. Motion and motionlessness, too, can be shelter: minute aquatic organisms, whose predators know them by the disturbance they make in the water, become cryptic by holding still. The same squid that first hides in the camouflage of protective coloration will, further threatened, jet swiftly away, leaving behind a shadow-body of ink: highly visible, substanceless decoy.

In the arts, the breadth of inventive disguise is much the same. To plunge one thing into the shape or nature of another is a fundamental gesture of creative insight, part of how we make for ourselves a world more expansive, deft, fertile, and startling in richness. The borrowing of attributes found in lyric image, metaphor, and parable is also one of the principles of sympathetic magic, used as a way to attempt to nudge the hand of chance or fate. A small example can be found in the Hoxne Hoard, a collection of late-fourth-century Roman treasure dug up in a Suffolk field in 1992 by a man who set out looking for a friend's lost hammer. Among the objects is the silver handle of a pouring vessel in the shape of a leaping tigress, heavy teats swelling down from the arc of her body. The sight pleases in its unexpected grace. It is also a promise of abundance— the principle of correspondence proposes that the vessel with such a handle, like the body of an actual nursing tigress, will not be emptied without that emptying causing it to refill.

To see the tigress hiding within a handle, the handle waiting within the tigress, is to throw off the boundaries of the literal and recognize that even the simplest fragment of existence can carry multiple uses, possibilities, connections. The union, like all metaphor, brings revelation and addition, while it also covers, complicates, veils. Art amplifies intelligence: to experience the tiger's silver-doubled resonance is to join in the leap the mind must take toward a more sophisticated comprehension of the world. And that leap into new comprehension is also the difference between the more overt simile and the way a fully realized metaphor affects us—to say that a handle is "like a tiger" would merely perplex, but to make of a handle a bounding tigress is to enter the world of dreams, in which all things mysteriously conjoin.

"Our seeing is a mirror or a sieve," wrote Zbigniew Herbert, in a poem meditating upon the sense of touch. The statement is eight words long, yet to unfold its two alternative metaphors fully would require passage through neuroscience, epistemology, personal psychology, and the grief of the self's inadequacy before words. Aristotle, in his *Rhetoric,* alludes to the kinship between metaphor and riddle, calling each a source for the other. Not only does solving a riddle depend on the ability to think metaphorically, all metaphor preserves some flavor of a puzzle. A metaphor is language that simultaneously creates and solves its own riddle; within that minute explosion of mind is both expansion and release. Perhaps this is why riddles abound among the earliest poems in many traditions and why spiritual teaching so often partakes of the riddling: it is how the mind instructs itself in a more complex seeing. Probably the most famous of Western riddles is the one posed by the Sphinx and answered by Oedipus: "What is it that walks on four legs at morning, two at midday, three at evening?" The answer is "Man," a being who crawls as an infant, walks upright in adulthood, and uses a cane in old age. The latent meaning that follows quietly behind the Greek story, like a large dog at leashless heel, is this: Man is the creature who solves or fails to solve riddles. If he fails, he will die; if he succeeds, it will not release him from suffering, but he will be fully human. We build canes of the material stuff of the world, and of our lives, our thoughts, our cultures, our words, our wits.

Here is another small example, from the seventh-century Anglo-Saxon of Aldhelm, abbot of Malmesbury, author of a collection of 101 rhyming riddles:

> *Once I was water, filled with scaly fish.*
> *Fate fickled then, decreed another wish,*
> *and torment-plunged me to a fiery place.*
> *Now whitest ash-shine, bright snow, are my face.*

Aldhelm of Malmesbury
tr. by Jane Hirshfield

Even in this small quatrain about seawater's transformation into salt by fire, the hint of a full worldview—in the reference to Fate—is present. It is the nature of riddles, and of metaphors, to exceed their apparent terrain, to teach us also to exceed the apparent when we read them. In the koans of Zen, the curriculum is explicit: "Show me your face," one famous example requests, "before your parents were born."

☙

Mystery, secrecy, camouflage, silence, stillness, shadow, distance, opacity, withdrawal, namelessness, erasure, encryption, enigma, darkness, absence—these are the kaleidoscope names of the hidden, each carrying its particular description of something whose essence eludes describing. It is not surprising that the trope of hiddenness appears throughout the world's spiritual traditions. In some Sufi and Kabbalist traditions, the face of the divine is said to have hidden itself in the fragmented world. Certain Tibetan Buddhist sutras, called *termas,* are texts believed to have been hidden for future revelation, given into the care of the *naga* dragon deities living deep in the earth, oceans, or lakes, or left in caves for later discovery. It is easy to dismiss such stories, to think of them as charismatic and exotic confabulation. Then we remember the Dead Sea Scrolls, dating from the first centuries of the Christian era, found in a cave by two Bedouin shepherds in 1947 while searching for a lost goat. The similarly ancient Nag Hammadi Gnostic Gospels were buried in a meter-tall jar in another cave, and discovered in 1945 by Egyptian brothers hunting nitrate to fertilize their garden. The Paleolithic bison and horses of Lascaux were found by four boys and their dog—they were looking in one version of the story for treasure, in another for the dog.

It is possible to begin to see a theme here: people go looking for one thing, and find another. A lost hammer leads to a Roman treasure, a lost goat to a cache of spiritual texts. Perhaps, for something to be found, the only thing that matters is that there be searching—certainly that is the way in the writing of poems.

Riddle-mind, whether spiritual, psychological, or secular, awakens a long-strided intelligence, breaking thought loose from the habitual and the stolid. This may explain why the following poem by Jack Gilbert brings so much pleasure—it is a handle revealing its tigress. To read it is to feel restored to some original, partially forgotten complexity and fullness of being—though the poem shows also how often, as with Odysseus, such restoration must be arrived at by an arduous passage through longing, failure, and loss.

THE FORGOTTEN DIALECT OF THE HEART

How astonishing it is that language can almost mean,
and frightening that it does not quite. Love, *we say,*
God, *we say,* Rome *and* Michiko, *we write, and the words*
get it wrong. We say bread *and it means according*
to which nation. French has no word for home,
and we have no word for strict pleasure. A people
in northern India is dying out because their ancient
tongue has no words for endearment. I dream of lost
vocabularies that might express some of what
we no longer can. Maybe the Etruscan texts would
finally explain why the couples on their tombs
are smiling. And maybe not. When the thousands
of mysterious Sumerian tablets were translated,
they seemed to be business records. But what if they
are poems or psalms? My joy is the same as twelve
Ethiopian goats standing silent in the morning light.
O Lord, thou art slabs of salt and ingots of copper,
as grand as ripe barley lithe under the wind's labor.

Her breasts are six white oxen loaded with bolts
of long-fibered Egyptian cotton. My love is a hundred
pitchers of honey. Shiploads of thuya are what
my body wants to say to your body. Giraffes are this
desire in the dark. Perhaps the spiral Minoan script
is not a language but a map. What we feel most has
no name but amber, archers, cinnamon, horses and birds.

Jack Gilbert

·

Something in us awakens and breathes more deeply when it feels the world supple in its transformations and meanings. This is the leavening in the words of the French poet Paul Éluard: "There is another world, but it is in this one." It is also the leavening in any piece of literature worth reading. Only words that enlarge the realm of the possible merit borrowing our attention from the world of the actual and the living: they will return us to it restored to the knowledge of a malleability and amplitude we may have forgotten.

Another of hiding's faces is that of hiding in plain sight. This is what the walking-stick insect is doing, what certain forms of irony do as well. Some measure of open hiding can be found in most good poems: poetic meaning almost always pulls in two directions, the unspoken evening shadow lengthening out behind seeming noon light. Some might suggest that this is the only form of hiding—one Chinese Zen practitioner, known to us only as Layman

P'ang's daughter, said in the eighth century, "All the teachings of the ancient masters can be found on the tips of the ten thousand grasses."

If something is to be felt as deeply true, the psyche wants it to have always been there; newly minted truths lack the authority of history and tested abidance. For this reason, the translators of the King James Bible deliberately set its diction into that of a time predating their own. Poets, writers, painters, and the psyche itself are frequently forgers—in both that word's meanings—claiming to make only what already exists.

It is impossible to think long about hiddenness without coming into the gravitational field of Edgar Allan Poe, and impossible to contemplate open hiding without arriving at "The Purloined Letter." Twice in that story, an incriminating letter is concealed by being left baldly in view; twice the device succeeds for a time, then ultimately fails. Part of Poe's purpose, in this story and elsewhere, is to instruct the reader in how an extraordinary discernment may see what ordinary discernment does not: not by force of conquest, but by making of hiddenness an ally. The lesson appears in miniature at the story's start, when the narrator and his friend Dupin are smoking companionably in Dupin's library in the gathering dusk. They have been silent together for an hour or more when the Prefect of the Parisian police, identified only by the initial G——, arrives. "We had been sitting in the dark," the narrator reports, "and Dupin now arose for the purpose of lighting a lamp, but sat down again, without doing so, upon G——'s saying that he had called to consult upon official business 'If it is any point requiring reflection,' observed Dupin, as he forbore to enkindle the wick, 'we shall examine it to better purpose in the dark.'"

Even at the most seemingly superficial level, Poe's stories are cat-and-mouse toyings with hiddenness, with information given and withheld. Throughout his works, for no apparent reason, amid a flood of offered details some small piece of information will be denied. Yet the device is not accidental or arbitrary; Poe's use of it, looked at closely, is a master class in rhetoric's power to persuade without saying directly. By implying, for instance, that the Prefect is a person in need of discreet allusion, namable only by his initial, Poe contrives to make G——, and so the whole story, appear not fictive, but true. "Why," the reader subliminally thinks, "would a fictional person require protection from being named?" Obscurity, then, creates a semblance of the three-dimensional real, with its directional light and cast shadows: in a world where something must be hidden, what is revealed must exist. (The reader's relationship to the story shifts as well; he or she becomes an insider, one trusted to recognize the person behind the hint. "Ah yes," the reader thinks, "Prefect G——, I have met him before." As she has, in "The Murders in the Rue Morgue.")

Poe's stratagem points toward a larger dynamic: hiddenness in itself has meaning and gives weight. In the psyche's archetypal reaches, treasure and secret align. Concealed in attic or vault, the essence of treasure is that it is sequestered, and neither easily come by nor easily kept—consider the pyramids' riches, protected by both mass and legends of curse. Consider *Beowulf*'s dragon's buried hoard, Fort

Knox, and Wagner's *Rheingold.* The immaterial borrows the outer world's patterns, and so inspiration, too, is often placed into the trope of a preserving, unseen gestation. Robert Frost states it with his customary pith: "One has to be secret in order to secrete."

Just as deliberate concealment conveys the sense of the real, the presence of mystery increases the conviction that there must be meaning. The elusive—in life, in literature—raises knowledge-lust in us the way a small, quick movement raises the hunting response in a cat. And the elusive exists at multiple levels. To turn again to Poe, the story "The Gold Bug" investigates less the finding of actual treasure—though that in part gives the story its surface drive—than the transformations of being by which it occurs. What engages the narrator's passion is not buried gemstones, but the process of arriving at clarity, at something revealed. Accident—Trickster's contribution—also plays its part: a piece of paper with directions to a treasure written in invisible ink is exposed by chance to heat. (Cold preserves, heat transforms, in the psyche as in the physical world.) Still, by halfway through the story, the treasure has already been dug up and savored. As in "The Purloined Letter," in which the letter is returned to its rightful owner long before the tale's conclusion, the overt outcome to the overt mystery is, for Poe, a trifle, tossed to the reader in passing. The real pleasure—in murder mysteries, detective stories, comedies, tragedies of error, and poems—is found in grappling with an existence that has not been made simple. Riddle-raising and riddle-unraveling stories appeal because they stand against and correct the impulse in us toward an overly rational abstraction. The savor of mystery teaches that details matter.

Poe did not want the merely real: he sought something both less and more than what can be arrived at by ordinary perception. "The Descent into the Maelstrom," "A Cask of Amontillado," "The Pit and the Pendulum," scar the psyche more deeply than the more straightforward tales of terror because they are neither reducible to allegory nor plausibly true. The raven of his famous poem is never explained. Poe is a writer entranced only with the shadows in Emerson's fir trees' boughs. "The mere imitation, however accurate, of what *is* in Nature," Poe wrote, "entitles no man to the sacred name of 'Artist.' . . . We can, at any time, double the true beauty of an actual landscape by half closing our eyes as we look at it. The naked Senses sometimes see too little—but then *always* they see too much."

.

Most good poems hold some part of their thoughts in invisible ink. Such words, unlike Poe's map, need not be exposed to be perceived. The unexpressed can at times affect the reader more strongly than what is explicit, precisely because it has not been narrowed by conscious accounting. Lyric poetry rests on a fulcrum of said and unsaid, and lives by clarities and complexities alloyed in mysteriously counterbalancing proportion. Within a good poem of intricate surface, more often than not, some large and simple unspoken gesture can be found; within a good poem apparently simple, more often than not, are behind-stage resonances, overtones, hidden knowledges, doublings back. As one Japanese proverb states, "Even the reverse has a reverse." W. H. Auden called great art, "clear thinking about complex feelings." Auden's own "Musée des Beaux Arts" serves well to examine how this complexity works, and how something entirely unexpressed can be nonetheless felt in a poem:

MUSÉE DES BEAUX ARTS

About suffering they were never wrong,
The Old Masters: how well they understood
Its human position: how it takes place
While someone else is eating or opening a window or just walking
*   dully along;*
How, when the aged are reverently, passionately waiting
For the miraculous birth, there always must be
Children who did not specially want it to happen, skating
On a pond at the edge of the wood:
They never forgot
That even the dreadful martyrdom must run its course
Anyhow in a corner, some untidy spot
Where the dogs go on with their doggy life and the torturer's horse
Scratches its innocent behind on a tree.

In Brueghel's Icarus, *for instance: how everything turns away*
Quite leisurely from the disaster; the ploughman may
Have heard the splash, the forsaken cry,
But for him it was not an important failure; the sun shone
As it had to on the white legs disappearing into the green
Water; and the expensive, delicate ship that must have seen

Something amazing, a boy falling out of the sky,
Had somewhere to get to and sailed calmly on.

W. H. Auden

The poem seems at first straightforward. It begins with a general statement about suffering, then extends and expands that idea with several examples. But the poem does not sit on this surface level of point and illustration; it plunges toward depth as quickly as its falling boy plunges into the sea. At the risk of ignoring Robert Frost's useful warning that explication consists of "saying a poem over again, only worse," let us try to expose a little of this poem's more subterranean effects and sleight-of-hand power.

First, there is its sound-making. Rhymes and half rhymes thread their way through Auden's words like an irregular flash of gold thread—the full rhymes of "wrong" and "along," "waiting" and "skating," but also the subtler and at times visually buried inter-callings of "tree" and "leisurely," "failure" and "water," "shone" and "on." There is also the rhythm: long-strided, complex sentences, extended by semicolon, colon, comma. On a drumbeat of what feels a kind of musically impeccable reasoning, the poem thinks its way forward, into a new understanding. Even a non-English speaker, listening to this poem, could hear in it the measures of thought's consideration and fulfillment.

But what is that conclusion? Paraphrased, it's pancake thin: "Mundane life goes on, it swallows even the most extraordinary individual disaster." Not an uninteresting statement, but one with none of the resonance of

Auden's poem—not its sense of a revelation wrung from the world by deep contemplation, not its undertow grief. At this level, one might call the poem a simplicity dressed in complex clothes. Even that quality, though, contributes to the poem's ultimate effect. The complicating rhetorical frame, for instance, works both to augment the poem's authority and to deepen its thinking's time and cultural ground, by placing the central proposition not in the mind of the author, but in the thoughts of the Old Master painters. What might have been felt individual opinion is now communal, time-tempered wisdom. The particularity and detail of the alluded-to paintings, with their precisely rendered images of children skating on frozen ponds, the dogs and horses, plowing peasant farmers, and high-masted sailing ships, increases the poem's density and gravitas as well. Embedded in actual life, the idea of suffering is not an abstraction. We feel the rub of the itchy, long-dead horse against the tree, and with it the rub of our own small, finite, and mortal human existence against the world of others, animate and inanimate, transient and lasting. The effect of this poem is to scour the reader with the knowledge the paintings hold also: that a moment occurs only once, in the vastness of time. And so, reading these lines, an unexpected feeling, half tenderness, half terror, floods the heart: Aristotle's classic, cleansing catharsis.

There is something else though, I think, an extra pressure of meaning that infuses the poem by having first infused its writer. Even if the reader does not consciously realize a subtext is there, its weight and presence affect us. "Musée des Beaux Arts" was written in December 1938.

Auden, an Englishman with no small sense of history, had been living not long before in Berlin. Months earlier, the annexation of Austria had occurred, and the ceding of the Czech Sudetenland to Germany had just been negotiated in Munich. We must guess that Auden knew something of the terrors already in place, had some sense of the increase of terror about to come, and knew how it, too, might be swallowed by the oblivious world. That, I believe, is the true source of the poem's bitterness, the serrated knife edge one feels when reading it through. This poem is as chillingly politically prescient as its more prominent sibling, Auden's "September 1, 1939." The weight of impotent foreknowledge leans as heavily as an unseen draft horse into this seemingly calm examination of centuries-old art.

As the making and solving of riddles creates intelligence, so a distinctive self is created by navigating a path between the desire for a sheltering hiddenness and the wish to both see and be seen. In the Hebrew Bible, the ability to give birth and the covering fig leaf—the creative capacity and shame's impulse toward hiding its sources—arrive together. Descartes, devoted to discovery, was in his own life deeply secretive, and claimed for his motto *Bene vixit, bene qui latuit:* "He who lives well lives well hidden."

Yet the British psychologist D. W. Winnicott described the dilemma of childhood by saying "It is a joy to be hidden, but a disaster not to be found." (One could say the same of certain writers' minute meaning-clues and interweavings: they are set down with full awareness that only the most alert readers will ever make them conscious, yet in hope that a followable trail has been laid.) Freud posited the adult self as riddled with secret chambers not knowable at all, expressing themselves only in dreams, tongue-slips, irrational behaviors, illness. We are psychologically, as biologically, made visible by our desires. And display itself can also conceal, as the raised quills of a porcupine not only warn but also disguise the true size of its actual body. This is the sleight of hand of the sequined magician, the strategy of the shy person who cultivates the persona of outrageous dress, covering the fear of strangeness with further strangeness.

Revelation as a journey toward the fully individuated self is described in the myth of Psyche, the girl taken in marriage by Eros after his mother, Venus, already jealous of Psyche's great beauty, has sent him to do her harm. Fearing his mother's increased anger, Eros keeps the marriage secret; he visits his new bride only in darkness, warning her of disaster should she try to discover who he is. (An odd displacement of secrecy, this, as it is Venus from whom the transgression must be concealed.) Their joyous if half-unconscious arrangement might have continued unbroken, but convinced by jealous sisters that her unseen husband must be a monster, one night Psyche carries a lamp to the bed where he sleeps. As she stands breathless before his beauty, a drop of hot lamp oil falls onto his shoulder, and the god awakens and flees. In the aftermath of that revelation, Psyche's trials begin—aided throughout, it is worth remembering, by powers that lie outside the scope of both conscious intelligence and intention: ants, reeds, other gods, a bird.

Perhaps one message to be taken from the many myths that speak of a broken concealment is the need for tact. In life, as in literature and myth, the desire to strip reality down to some bare and blunt truth reflects delusion, hubris, or reductionism's inedible dust. As there is a connection between modesty, the generative, and a clear-seeing compassion, there is one also between hubris and an ensuing blindness. What is bared without sufficient respect may not be bearable, or bearable only at enormous cost. And still, a paradox is here. Until she engages the world with oil lamp and open eyes, Psyche cannot become what her name has come to mean: a soul, a being fully engaged in the living through of her own deep existence.

At other times, though, the hidden's job may be to remain fully hidden. Definitiveness can diminish; an alert unknowing keeps open the range of what may be possible. Richard Hugo counseled young poets never to ask a question in their poems to which they knew the answer. Chekhov advised his brother, "Art doesn't provide answers, it can only formulate questions correctly." Certain jokes, teaching tales, and koans share a similar intention: to dismantle all certainties concerning a person's place in the world.

In one traditional Hasidic story, a man tortured by doubt travels a great distance hoping to ask a famous teacher his question. At first, the teacher's disciples will not allow the stranger into the study house, but one day he slips in, approaches the rebbe, and speaks: "Venerable

Rebbe, forgive me for disturbing you, but I have traveled many weeks and waited many days for the chance to ask you a question that has troubled me all my life." "What is your question?" the teacher responds. The man asks, "What is the essence of truth?" The rebbe looks at his visitor for a moment, rises from his chair, approaches, slaps him hard, then withdraws again to his books. The shocked and affronted questioner retreats to a tavern across the road, bitterly and loudly complaining of his mistreatment. One of the teacher's disciples, overhearing, takes pity and explains: "The rebbe's slap was given you in great kindness, to teach you this: never surrender a good question for a mere answer."

When the world is looked at from the condition of asking, each thing is seen both for itself, just as it is, and as the holder of the immeasurable mysteries good questions unlatch. A world—or book—that is felt to contain the hidden is inexhaustible to the imagination. New possibilities surround any moment that presents itself as question rather than answer. It's the inability to be known or explicated completely that infuses aliveness into good poems—they become, as the poet Donald Hall has written, houses with a secret room at the center, the place in which all that cannot be paraphrased is stored. The room can never be opened to ordinary habitation, yet its presence changes the house. And in truth, the unopenable room does not reside in the outward data of the world, or in the words of the poem: it resides in us.

In the imagery of Islam, paradise is a walled garden; the Hebrew word from which our English "paradise" comes is *pardes*, whose ordinary meaning is orchard. Kabbalists map how an orchard becomes the dwelling place of the sacred by showing the hidden meaning that resides in each of its letters. "P" stands for *peshat*, the mind that sees the world literally; "r" for *remez*, the understanding of allusion and metonymy; "d" is for *derash*, metaphoric or symbolic interpretation; and "s" for *sod*—"secret." There is no paradise, no place of true completion, that does not include within its walls the unknown.

Hiddenness is the ballast in the ship's keel, the great underwater portion of a life that steadies the rest. The thirteenth-century Zen teacher Eihei Dogen described its weight of presence thus: "There are mountains hidden in treasures. There are mountains hidden in swamps. There are mountains hidden in the sky. There are mountains hidden in mountains. There are mountains hidden in hiddenness. This is complete understanding."

To store understanding in the hidden, the unseen and unsaid, can be rhetoric's wisdom as well. What cannot be conveyed in words can be carried inside a basket of silence. And so, in the fourth "Georgic," when Virgil tells the story of Orpheus and Eurydice, the poet leaves undescribed the song by which Orpheus persuades Hades to allow Eurydice to return to the world of the living. The poem offers instead the song's effect on those who hear what the reader cannot. The snakes of the Furies' hair lift motionless, spellbound. The three-headed guard dog Cerberus stands with all three mouths open, forgetting to bark.

.

The real is shy of words, and rightly. As Ted Hughes wrote, "Like Cordelia in King Lear, perhaps the more sure of itself truth is, the more doubtful it is of the adequacy of words." Bewilderment before questions of speech and silence, ambivalence before the experience both of seeing and of being seen, run through the words of many writers. Let us close then with two poems by the early twentieth-century Greek poet C. P. Cavafy that speak to the two sides of hiddenness, making a compelling case for each in turn.

The first concerns concealment as obstacle and grief. It may emerge from the poet's relationship to his sexuality, a theme that permeates many of Cavafy's poems, though it is never explicitly named. Still, such an interpretation may be reductive; the poem may equally speak of something even more complexly unsayable. In either case, its reticence is inseparable from its meaning.

HIDDEN THINGS

From all I did and all I said
let no one try to find out who I was.
An obstacle was there that changed the pattern
of my actions and the manner of my life.
An obstacle was often there
to stop me when I'd begin to speak.
From my most unnoticed actions,
my most veiled writing—
from these alone will I be understood.
But maybe it isn't worth so much concern,
so much effort to discover who I really am.

Later, in a more perfect society,
someone else made just like me
is certain to appear and act freely.

C. P. Cavafy
tr. by Edmund Keeley and Philip Sherrard

The second poem offers an alternative view, an argument on behalf of hiddenness. It attests to the importance of a thing done not for others' regard or praise but for the sake of the psyche's own existence, known in solitude, neither the subject nor object of others' attention. The poem speaks, that is, to the importance of the imagination's own exhilaration in making and of a life's worth, inalienable in simply existing.

FOR THE SHOP

He wrapped them up carefully, neatly,
in expensive green silk.
Roses of rubies, lilies of pearl,
violets of amethyst: beautiful according to his taste,
to his desire, his vision—not as he saw them in nature
or studied them. He'll leave them in the safe,
examples of his bold, his skillful work.
Whenever a customer comes into the shop,
he brings out other things to sell—first class ornaments:
bracelets, chains, necklaces, rings.

C. P. Cavafy
tr. by Edmund Keeley and Phillip Sherrard

Some may believe that a creation unseen is wasted, its maker selfish. But what I have been trying to examine today is the way that those bold, idiosyncratic jewel-flowers, even concealed, still affect. They change the shop, they change the jeweler, they change even the customer who leaves with his ordinary bracelet and ring. The thought that something we cannot see, of unsurpassable skill and unimaginable form, exists in the back room's locked safe—isn't this, for any artist, for any person, an irresistible hope, beautiful and disturbing as the distant baying of Thoreau's lost hound that tells us, not least, that the mysteries of distance are endless?

CHAPTER FIVE

Uncarryable Remainders:
Poetry and Uncertainty

Chaos, Hesiod wrote, is the progenitor of all other beings and things—gods, animals, humans, rocks, stars, waters, trees, winds. Existence, it seems, takes root in ground so unfathomable it can only be given a name and left behind. In one place, the name is Chaos, in another, the Big Bang. In one much-told story, the name is "turtles." The story appears, appropriately, in differing versions. An astronomer, or a physicist, or a philosopher, has just finished lecturing on the structure of the cosmos. When he asks for questions, an elderly woman raises her hand. "Professor James," she says—or Russell, or Sagan, or Dyson—"you are quite an interesting young man, but you've got it all wrong. Everyone knows the universe rests on the back of a very large tortoise." The speaker answers gently, "And what does the tortoise rest on?" The woman replies, "Oh, clever, young man, very clever—but it's turtles all the way down."

One of the penalties and graces of consciousness is waking each day to the awareness that the future cannot be predicted, that the universe's foundation rests on an incomprehensible receding, that bewilderment, caprice, and the unknowable are among the most faithful companions of any life. Mostly, it seems, we go on by inventing a story. Yet no story completely suffices, and eventually the turtle appears in its runic shell, munching some contemplative bit of lettuce.

For those willing to let themselves feel it, any story leaves behind an uneasiness, sometimes at the center, other times at the edge of perception, and like the remainder left over in a problem in long division, it must be carried. Literature's work, and particularly poetry's, is in part to take up that residue and remnant, to find a way to live amid and alongside the uncertain. Plato banished poets from his republic in part because he thought poetry escapist, that it dulls the desire for truth by the hypnosis of beauty. But good poetry, as we've begun to see, doesn't in fact allay anxiety with answers—it startles its reader out of the general trance, enlarging a bearable reality by means of a close-paid attention to attention's own ground.

Keats described poetry's relationship to the unknowable in a letter written on the winter solstice of 1817. In it he famously ascribed poetic genius to a kind of anti-talent. "Negative Capability," he called it—"that is when man is capable of being in uncertainties, Mysteries, doubts, without any irritable reaching after fact & reason." A century later, William Empson echoed Keats's insight when he named ambiguity the central quality of poetic beauty.

Awareness of the fragility of intention and hope; a steady dose of doubt and self-doubt; knowledge of the Heisenbergian effects of the observer's own existence—these identifiers of human consciousness are also markers for what we call "literature," as opposed to those forms of writing that inform, dictate, flatter, plead, terrorize, lure, or simplistically entertain. Awareness of uncertainty signals the entrance of human individuality into the consciousness of the commons. What we think of as "art" goes further: it makes the encounter with the uncertain a thing to be sought. Death-fear is turned into *Gilgamesh,* doubt of other and self becomes *Hamlet,* and our human relationship to what cannot be known is permanently altered. That anxiety, grief, and the abysses of chaos can be lured into beauty and meaning, and into the freedom such transmutation itself brings, is no small part of literature's power, whether experienced as Aristotelian catharsis or in more subtle forms. The point is not resolution, but knowing.

Knowing and not-knowing, uncertainty and certainty, were much on Keats's mind during that early-nineteenth-century winter. A month earlier, he wrote in another letter, "I am certain of nothing but the heart's affections and the truth of imagination—what the imagination seizes as beauty must be truth—whether it existed before or not." By mid-January, he wrote: "There's nothing stable in the world—uproar's your only music." The eighteenth century's Enlightenment confidence in rationality and control has been thoroughly discarded, yet the paralysis of Shakespeare's Danish prince is equally absent. In place of objective knowledge and permanence, Keats puts his faith in the chameleon interior life: quick on its feet, subjective, permeable, eager to be seized by the ground it finds itself on. (If Hamlet had had the Negative Capability of his creator, he might have lived to become the fine king Fortinbras declares he would have been.)

To exchange certainty for praise of mystery and doubt is to step back from hubris and stand in the receptive, both vulnerable and exposed. The Heian-era Japanese poet Izumi Shikibu expressed a similar understanding in one of her tanka. Written around the year 1000, its thirty-one syllables—in the original Japanese—agree to, even invite, Keats's instability and "uproar":

> *Although the wind*
> *blows terribly here,*
> *moonlight*
> *also leaks between the roof planks*
> *of this ruined house.*

Izumi Shikibu

tr. by Jane Hirshfield and Mariko Aratani

Shikibu's poem reminds its reader that the moon's beauty, and also the Buddhist awakening frequently signaled in Japanese poetry by images of moonlight, will come to a person only if the full range of events and feelings are allowed in as well. Permeability cannot be provisional. It is impossible to know what will enter if the house of the solidified and defended self is breached, and ruin is not a condition any person willingly seeks. Still, those gaps in the roof planks—not the assigned doors, the expected windows— are the opening through which the luminous arrives.

We tend to think of good poems as preserving and transmitting some knowledge, often hard won. And, as with Shikibu's tanka, they do. Yet poetry comes into being by the fracture of knowing and sureness—it begins not in understanding but in a willing, undefended meeting with whatever arrives. A person in need of answers will be a person assailed by questions, and the biographies of poets, like those of mystics, are filled with dark nights of the soul. The Polish poet Anna Świrszczyńska (called "Anna Swir" in some English translations) described with unflinching directness the bleakness of fundamentally unanswerable questions:

POETRY READING

I'm curled into a ball
like a dog
that is cold.

Who will tell me
why I was born,
why this monstrosity
called life.

The telephone rings. I have to give
a poetry reading.

I enter.
A hundred people, a hundred pairs of eyes.
They look, they wait.
I know for what.

I am supposed to tell them
why they were born,
why there is
this monstrosity called life.

Anna Swir

tr. by Czesław Miłosz and Leonard Nathan

Poetry often enacts the recovering of emotional and metaphysical balance, whether in an individual (primarily the lyric poem's task) or in a culture (the task of the epic). Yet to do that work, a poem needs to retain within its words some of the disequilibrium that called it forth, and to include when it is finished some sense also of uncomfortable remainder, the undissolvable residue carried over— disorder and brokenness are necessarily part of human wholeness. Anna Swir's poem is virtually all remainder. It refuses any idealization of poetic wisdom, any transformative lyric closure; it ends as it begins. And yet this poem does what good poems do: increases our sense of participation in the human. It counters isolation and meaninglessness, even while offering no replacement beyond its own presence. The satisfaction felt by its reader—and for me, Swir's poem does bring a considerable solace—comes in its reminder of the commonality of grief, perplexity, and the failure to comprehend or transcend. By drawing from what is so often the strategy of comedy—that is, by admitting the truth—the poem makes despair both lighter and more bearable. It does this by showing despair for what it is: a touchstone of any life spent without blinders.

Izumi Shikibu's tanka is not so different from this as it may first seem—if the reader doesn't grant the wind and leaking house their full severity, the poem's moonlight means nothing. The relationship between uncertainty and solace in these poems—as in life—is not curative; it is one of "also." And that is enough. Wallace Stevens called writing an act of self-preservation, the imagination pressing back against the inward-pressing real. This is less a wisdom coolly achieved than sleight of hand, a conjured aikido of language. The most serene works on the bookshelf are nonetheless in the lineage of Scheherazade's stories—art holding incoherence and death at bay by invention of beauty, detour, and suspense. This is Sartre's definition of genius: not a gift, but the escape a person invents in a desperate time.

Fear makes good ground for literature, it seems. The earliest recorded writing for which we know a historical author is Enheduanna's "Hymn to Inanna," composed in the midst of a savage Sumerian war. Over four millennia later, Virginia Woolf alluded to poetry's role during similar times. In the central section of *To the Lighthouse,* Woolf describes the effects of time on the Ramsays' summer cottage in the Hebrides—a house, like Izumi Shikibu's, going to ruin. Unvisited and untended, its wallpaper loosens; a shawl draped over a mounted boar's head comes free, corner by corner, over years; window frames, plaster, and roof shingles yield to the elements. In brief, bracket-held sentences, a series of revelations appear, each a small telegram interrupting the house's gradual fall into decay and disrepair—the family's eldest son, Andrew, is blown up by a shell on the fields of the Great War; the daughter Prue weds and then dies giving birth; Woolf slips the death of Mrs. Ramsay herself into a passing phrase. A more casual bit of information also appears: the Ramsays' house-guest poet, August Carmichael, has become an unexpected success. The novel explains it thus: "The war, people said, had revived their interest in poetry."

A lyric poem does not solve any outward dilemma; few answer any practical question, none refastens a single loose shingle to a house. As Auden wrote in his elegy for Yeats, "Poetry makes nothing happen." Yet when crisis requires a mode of negotiation with the chaos, entropy, and loss-terror that co-inhabit any human life, poems are turned toward, as a plant requiring its photosynthesized sugars turns toward the sun.

How to name where poetry's consoling powers may lie? One part can be found in what has already been seen in Anna Swir's poem: the sense of connection with others that good poems both emerge from and forge. In the simplest act of recognizing the imaginative, metaphoric, or narrative expression of another, you find yourself less lonely, more accompanied in this life. Another part may come in what the medieval alchemists called *solutio*—the process of making something workable and transformable by making it more fluid, whether in the physical or metaphysical realms. A difficult thing is "hard," we say; a mathematical answer arrived at is "solved." A good poem, then, is a solvent, a kind of WD-40 for the soul. This is the efficacy of Aristotle's catharsis. To feel oneself moved creates in itself an increase of freedom; outward circumstance is not the self's only definition when the imagination is present to press against it. Primo Levi described the exhilaration he felt at Auschwitz, when, sent with a fellow prisoner to fetch the midday soup, he attempted to reconstruct and recite for his partner (with whom he could scarcely communicate, not sharing a language) a canto from Dante. During those minutes, each recovered, however briefly, some sense of what it is to feel fully human.

Another facet of poetry's solace, related to *solutio*, is the increase of subtlety a good poem provides. Subtlety's etymological roots lie in loom-woven cloth. It is the name we give to thought that is both finely textured and ranging, able to bring disparate and multiple qualities into the unified, usable fabric of a new whole. The uncertain is subtlety's inscape: what is woven has—and needs—gaps. In subtle response, thought is stitched into place with its own undertows, opposites, and extensions, by a mind that questions and crosshatches its statements and feelings. Language itself is subtle by nature, multi-stranded of meaning—and what is good poetry if not language awake to its own powers? Even in poems that may seem to risk the didactic, if they are good poems, the buoying tact of the particular—whether in image, metaphor, music, or rhetoric—counterbalances certitude's lead weight. The recognition of language's skillful means extends far beyond literature. "Style," the physicist J. Robert Oppenheimer once said, "is the deference action pays to uncertainty. It is above all style through which power defers to reason."

Subtle thinking liberates its subject from the expected and assumed, from arrogance and the ordinary versions of what is thought true. On the scales of exact/inexact, accurate/inaccurate, right/wrong, true/false, subtlety steps to the side, slicing through cognitive categories as Chuang-Tzu's Taoist butcher sliced through the bones of the ox—finding the place where the joints fall open. Yet subtlety's openness is not to be confused with vagueness. Another exchange that followed a physicist's lecture comes to mind, this one involving Niels Bohr. Bohr had spoken on complementarity; afterwards, one listener asked what the complement of objective truth (*Wirklichkeit*) might be. "Clarity," Bohr replied.

Clarity is factuality that looks and feels more widely, letting in more than it knows it knows. It is as good a name as we may find for the combination of attentiveness, accuracy, and permeability to the subtle that we recognize in good poems. Some poems cannot be parsed at all, yet are consummately clear. The difference between Bohr's clarity and objectively graspable, paraphrasable fact is the difference between a live blue Morpho and one pinned for display. The dead butterfly's beauty is precisely what it was, yet even a black and white sumi ink sketch, in which almost everything is left out, might hold more of the insect's original vibrance. (Let us admit, though: an almost opposite interpretation of this interchange is equally plausible, one in which Bohr's point would be that reality is too complex to be captured by any clear understanding. Each reading of the dialogue holds its appeal; that both are possible illustrates uncertainty's scope.)

Walt Whitman points toward the aliveness and essential uncapturability of clear-seeing in another way, when he contrasts a narrow academic perception, entranced by schematics and numbers, with the way of looking—in the phrase "from time to time," it seems almost bashful—of the "unaccountable" self:

WHEN I HEARD THE LEARN'D ASTRONOMER

When I heard the learn'd astronomer,
When the proofs, the figures, were ranged in columns before me,
When I was shown the charts and diagrams, to add, divide, and
     measure them,
When I sitting heard the astronomer where he lectured with much
     applause in the lecture-room,
How soon unaccountable I became tired and sick,
Till rising and gliding out I wander'd off by myself,
In the mystical moist night-air, and from time to time,
Look'd up in perfect silence at the stars.

Walt Whitman

It is by and in its subtleties that a good poem is able both to answer uncertainty and to contain it. Here is an early poem by Czesław Miłosz, written in 1936 in Wilno, now Vilnius, in Lithuania. Nothing in it overtly resembles Whitman's poem, yet it offers its reader an experience recognizably near—a palpable enlargement of being; the slowed and deepened breath that comes with the release of fixed ideas for the more complex fullness and air of the real.

ENCOUNTER

We were riding through frozen fields in a wagon at dawn.
A red wing rose in the darkness.

And suddenly a hare ran across the road.
One of us pointed to it with his hand.

That was long ago. Today neither of them is alive,
Not the hare, nor the man who made the gesture.

O my love, where are they, where are they going,
The flash of a hand, streak of movement, rustle of pebble.
I ask, not out of sorrow, but in wonder.

Czesław Miłosz

tr. by Czesław Miłosz and Lillian Vallée

The poem transcribes bird, hare, a pointing hand, and behind them, the brutality that is transience. For resolution, it offers nothing beyond Miłosz's characteristic gesture of rescue: memory. There is no solving the central dilemma: time strips the world of all we have known and seen, and the knower and seer will not be exempt. And still, this small lyric carries large solace, and respects the ground of uncertainty by being one part answer, one part question, one part thrown-open window. Its "answer" may be described as the honoring of particularity and remembrance; its question is overt ("O my love, where are they, where are they going"); and the window—which escapes precise quotation, being opening rather than presence—might be the way that a landscape of frozen winter fields and a diction of plain reportage somehow turn, in changing to the direct, vocative-address grammar of the last stanza, into a tenderness surpassing ordinary grief, ordinary loss. This poem doesn't diminish time's pillagings by simple protest—it is instead a wagon traveling outside ego's domain, like Whitman stepping outside the lecture hall to the hall of stars.

The making of good poetry entails control; it also requires surrender and a light hand. A genuine art lives somewhere between the divination bones and the dice. That is, it lives along that exploration and geological fault line that has to do with which aspects of our lives we can know, which we cannot, and the spirit and tools with which we engage the question. We travel this line by taking aim with the whole body, the whole life, and then letting go, committing ourselves to the toss.

Some early divination bones and certain early dice (according to magician and historian of magic Ricky Jay, some six-thousand-year-old dice found in Egyptian tombs may have already been loaded) were both made of astragali—the squarish heel bones of hooved animals, especially antelopes and sheep. But the role that dice and divination play in the psyche is not the same. Divination, however rudimentary its premises, is the beginning of science: a tool for experimental observation, the examined bones are a search for answers, for a verifiably predictable world.

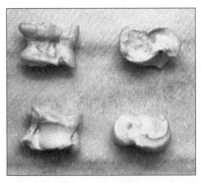

Bone dice

Oracle bones stand at the beginning of writing as well— in the mythological pantheon of China, as in Greece, the god of divination is also the god who brings writing into existence. Among the earliest remaining abstract markings are those notched upon bones; such artifacts go back at least fifteen thousand and possibly forty thousand years. To imagine the moment of discovery is easy: a person about to discard a femur or rib notices the marks of the hunting axe, or perhaps a row of nicks and scrapings left by the flaked-stone butchering knife, and decides to add to the pattern. Bone, whose hardened calcium enables terrestrial fleetness, is transformed after death into something quite different: a way to make a record at once portable and lasting. The white surface becomes a first, glimmering intimation of paper.

Gamblers' dice are different: they do not search for a path toward the knowable or recordable, they search for risk. They are a reply tossed gamely—in both that word's senses—into the face of the uncertain. The terrain of dice is feeling, not truth. Faced with what cannot be known, the gambler's response is to take it on, as if chance could somehow be wrestled, charmed, winked at, conned. Spinning the wheel, wagering, playing the odds, we engage the unengageable and hope to move fate.

Gaming courts the experience of uncertainty as much as it contains it. This is true of poems as well. Luck and inspiration are siblings, if not twins. The sense of luck—which is what we call chance when it's felt as possessing its own capacity for will—is a state of grace: some hand, we feel, is turning the dice in our favor. The smile of the Muse feels much the same. Inspiration comes and goes on its own currents and whim.

True, a cluster of good dice-falls—if the dice are honest—is simply the laws of probability having their way. But inside the psyche, that phenomenon has its own resonance. Neurophysiological research into decision-making reveals that the higher the level of uncertainty, the greater the dopamine-driven pleasure response in the brain upon its successful resolution. It is no surprise, then, that every human culture has developed the taste for gambling. An optimistic relationship to the unknown and the random is evolutionarily useful—whether hunting a meal or a mate, a certain resilience in the face of delay and uncertainty is required.

Encounter with the unknown seems almost a nutrient in human life, as essential as certain amino acids—without it, the untested self falls into sleep, depression, boredom, and stupor. The trick then is discovering how much, and when, to admit the random, chaotic, unknowable, into our lives—if, that is, we are among those who have the privilege of choice at all. It is also a matter of balance. The child at the mercy of an incomprehensible world requires reassurance; the adult, stalled in the familiar, may require an opposite prod. In a situation where nothing is new or changed, the repertory of experience will be confirmed but not expanded. As in ecological zones, periphery and boundary are where diversity and transformation lie—in art, in science, and in the day-to-day experience of a life, whether the renovation sought is of thought, feeling, or technique. Too much familiarity asks no attention; too much that is new cannot be comprehended at all.

Pursuit made without guarantee is in itself an innate, paradoxical pleasure, one that allows a writer or painter to persevere, even if externally unrewarded, for years. The wagered hope, the adrenaline risk of failure, are themselves part of the lure. Any artist seeking a true discovery, like any person seeking an unplacid life, must be willing to stand in harm's way—behind the door there may be a lady, there may be a tiger.

A story by Jorge Luis Borges, lover of tigers, comes to mind. The narrator of "The Lottery in Babylon" describes a society in which a lottery has expanded beyond its usual form to govern every aspect of life. The drawn ticket subjects a person to potential impoverishment as much as potential prosperity, affects societal role along with financial status. A person might go from proconsul to slave, from thief to priest, as the drawing of the lots decrees. The result—since the Company in charge of the lottery functions invisibly—is a world exactly like our own, but compressed, steepened, "saturated," as the narrator puts it, "with chance." "I have known," he says, "what the Greeks do not know, incertitude." The sentence is spoken with pride. Those who think the Company fictitious are branded heretic, and fools: for Borges's imagined Babylonians, a world believed governed by secret drawings is more alive and desirable than one that is not. To feel is to be at risk, and to be at risk is to feel.

·

Like an animal hunted as much for the challenge as for the meat or pelt, artistic masterpieces come into the world by hybrid means. Great painting, plays, novels, poems, are part talent, part effort, part training, part cultural context—but also part luck, part inspiration, part the willingness of the maker to offer him- or herself up to chance. Change is saturated with chance in all its phases.

From an asteroid collision to errors in genetic transcription, evolution is driven by accident, mishap, mistake. Transcription errors have their way in poems as well. Every writer has experienced the intention to set down one word, but then accidentally writing another, and recognizing at once that the wrong word is better—more accurate, more surprising. Working in rhyme and meter is throwing the word-dice in much the same hope. A statement is made without knowing where it will lead, and the end word of the line must then summon from the pool of all possible words one similar to itself, yet not perfectly so. Through the play of imperfect replication, thought—like biological life— evolves in unexpected directions: uncertainty both courted and contained. The process extends even to typographical error. The novelist Malcolm Lowry wrote a small and perfect poem on this phenomenon, the final work of his life:

STRANGE TYPE

I wrote "in the dark cavern of our birth."
The printer had it tavern, which seems better.
But herein lies the subject of our mirth,
Since on the next page death appears as dearth.
So it may be that God's word was distraction,
Which to our strange type appears destruction,
Which is bitter.

Malcolm Lowry

Poems, if they are good at all, hold knowledges elusive and multiple, unsayable in any other form. Resonant, fragrant, traveling more than one direction at a time, poetic speech escapes narrowing abstraction and reification as richly as does life itself. This is why lyric poems are so rife, as Lowry's is, with irony—good poems undercut their own yearning to say one thing well, because to say one thing only is not to say enough. Over-certainty and single-mindedness irritate as well as bore; the idea that one can know what is right, or that a general truth is possible, affronts the true complexity of the real. The Portuguese poet Fernando Pessoa captured this in a compact quatrain written under the heteronym of Alberto Caeiro:

THEY SPOKE TO ME OF PEOPLE, AND OF HUMANITY

They spoke to me of people, and of humanity.
But I've never seen people, or humanity.
I've seen various people, astonishingly dissimilar,
Each separated from the next by an unpeopled space.

Fernando Pessoa
tr. by Richard Zenith

Each time I read this poem, I feel an enormous relief. It is Whitman walking out of the lecture hall, or Yehuda Amichai's more contemporary version of the same impulse:

A GREAT TRANQUILITY: QUESTIONS AND ANSWERS

The people in the painfully bright auditorium
spoke about religion
in the life of contemporary man
and about God's place in it.

People spoke in excited voices
as they do at airports.
I walked away from them:
I opened an iron door marked "Emergency"
and entered into
a great tranquility: Questions and Answers.

Yehuda Amichai
tr. by Chana Bloch

How then does poetry speak with an appropriate humility and tact, in a world where over-certainty appears increasingly a threat to both humanity's and the planet's continuance? How accurately respect a world in which each moment requires a new and particular question, even as it answers the last's? There are, I suspect, four basic strategies. One is Malcolm Lowry's alternative to destruction—distraction. We might at first think this an act of denial—a whistling in the dark—but more kindly and fully, it is the choice to survive; to live "as if," and go on with the large and small affairs of a life, its loves, labors, and the ordinary pleasures of clean sheets and slow-cooked soups. This strategy is the difference between a Dutch *vanitas* painting, with its overt skull, and the painted landscape showing a winter village, its pond thick with skaters. Whatever lies under the pond's ice, joy is above it. As in the moment-to-moment conduct of a life itself, the largest portion of poems fall into this class. They do not concern themselves with certainty or uncertainty, their business is elsewhere. Yet they bow toward uncertainty's broadening directives, as all good art does: they do not overinsist, their beauty is made in the chiaroscuro of ambiguity, their windows are open, their skaters glide on meltable ice and in the company of their own shadows.

A second strategy is directness, an open-eyed agreement—to make one's peace with things as they are and love the world as transient, fallible, frail. This is the approach of the poem, uncanny of aptness, that appeared in the first issue of *The New Yorker* published after September 11, 2001. "Try to praise the mutilated world," it begins. "Remember June's long days, the wild strawberies, drops of wine, the dew. The nettles that methodically overgrow/the abandoned homesteads of exiles." Adam Zagajewski's lines were written before the terrorists struck, yet the poem's fragile tenderness in the midst of destruction was precisely the medicine needed in those stunned days, antidote to both fundamentalism and fear. Few poems have served such an immense and immediate hunger for some sayable response to uncarryable knowledge.

A short lyric by the Roman poet Horace provides an earlier example of this stance of direct, unsimplifying acceptance:

I, II

Leucon, no one's allowed to know his fate,
Not you, not me: don't ask, don't hunt for answers

In tea leaves or palms. Be patient with whatever comes.
This could be our last winter, it could be many
More, pounding the Tuscan Sea on these rocks:
Do what you must, be wise, cut your vines
And forget about hope. Time goes running, even
As we talk. Take the present, the future's no one's affair.

Horace

tr. by Burton Raffel

It's worth noticing that this strategy of directness often appears in those children's books whose reading endures for a lifetime. E. B. White's *Charlotte's Web* introduces a child to both the fearful concept of death and a path toward death's impossible accommodation. There is no pretense of superheroic immortality, no fantasy of permanent escape. The young pig Wilbur will someday die, as does his protector in the book, the spider Charlotte. But the knowledge of cycles is given, the presence of beloved companions, and the provision that verve, affection, and a generous imagination do matter; do clear, within transience, the preserving space in which life may go on, forgetting death, as it must for a spell of spell-bound time, almost entirely.

A third strategy, already glimpsed in Izumi Shikibu's tanka, is to make of uncertainty a home—a strategy not unlike standing out in the rain so long that, soaked through, a person grows once again warm; or if not warm, at least drenched to the point where no reason is left to seek shelter. Many contemporary poets work within the indeterminacy of meaning, but surely the most heartbreaking example is that of Paul Celan. His post-Holocaust poems, written in what he felt was the language of death—his home tongue of German—fracture their own words almost past speaking. Celan described himself as possessing a "true-stammered mouth," the world as a thing "to be stuttered after."

NO MORE SAND ART, no sand book, no masters.
Nothing on the dice. How many mutes?
Seventeen.

Your question—your answer.
Your song, what does it know?
Deepinsnow,
       Eepinnow,
          E-i-o.

Paul Celan
tr. by John Felstiner

The poem—entirely uncertainty, except for the enigmatically precise "seventeen"—erases itself from existence; yet that erasure itself is so powerful it engraves itself into memory with indelible force. John Felstiner, the poem's translator, has assembled critical speculation on some of the associative meanings—the seventeen mutes, one scholar suggests, might be "eighteen minus one," significant because in Hebrew numerology, eighteen spells "alive." No special knowledge is needed to feel the resonance of those unmarked dice, or the brunt of the final phrase's burial in its own enactment—but it chills to be reminded that words reduced only to their vowels in German are, in Hebrew, words that would no longer exist. In the life, as is well known, the silencing impulse prevailed— Celan committed suicide in 1970, at the age of forty-nine. But biography and art are not identical. His poems remain, adamant refusals of both certainty's easy speaking and silence.

It may be that all good poems reach toward the refuge of what can be said without betraying uncertainty's measure. Striking that lit-match balance is how poetry approaches our sense of the experienced real, which is equally wavering, fragile, and subject to changes of wind. In one poem, the solution might appear as spiritual amplitude tempered by mystery and shadow, in another as something absolutely basic and spare. This, I believe, is the fourth strategy by which poems engage the fundamental uncertainty of our lives: by a faithful reporting of only that which is present. Knowing nothing, a person can look to see what is here: ten fingers, ten toes, the experience of breathing, a chair. Pessoa wrote many poems in this stance of lucid, observing perception, in which any idea is recognized as only an idea, and so peripheral to the actual. Most, like the one given earlier, address that concept abstractly; a few, as here, provide a small demonstration of what it might be like to live in such a way:

THIS MAY BE THE LAST DAY OF MY LIFE

This may be the last day of my life.
I lifted my right hand to wave at the sun,
But I did not wave at it in farewell.
I was glad I could still see it—that's all.

Fernando Pessoa
tr. by Richard Zenith

"The Fly," by the Czech poet and immunologist Miroslav Holub, is also a poem of a simply recorded, imagined present. It addresses itself to uncertainty with indirect but unexpected force—as any honest describing of what happens (perhaps necessarily?) must:

THE FLY

She sat on a willow-trunk
watching
part of the battle of Crécy,
the shouts,
the gasps,
the groans,
the tramping and the tumbling.

During the fourteenth charge
of the French cavalry
she mated

with a brown-eyed male fly
from Vadincourt.

She rubbed her legs together
as she sat on a disemboweled horse
meditating
on the immortality of flies.

With relief she alighted
on the blue tongue
of the Duke of Clervaux.

When silence settled
and only the whisper of decay
softly circled the bodies

and only
a few arms and legs
still twitched jerkily under the trees,
she began to lay her eggs
on the single eye
of Johann Uhr,
the Royal Armourer.

And thus it was
that she was eaten by a swift
fleeing
from the fires of Estrées.

Miroslav Holub
tr. by George Theiner

While assembling these thoughts, I turned again to biologist Michael Dickinson, whose research investigates decision-making in *drosophila,* fruit flies. He wrote back:

I think the magnitude of uncertainty, U, is expressed well mathematically, as:

$$U = abs(I / (C - B)),$$

where *I* is the perceived impact of a decision, estimates *C* and *B* are the cost and benefits of the decision, and *abs* denotes absolute value (angst over things we decide to do is just as painful as angst over things we decide not to do). The direct relationship with impact is reasonably clear—we generally don't sweat the stuff that doesn't matter. Door number one or door number three: big impact. The lady or the tiger: big impact. "Would you like fresh cracked pepper?": little impact. The denominator is much more interesting; uncertainty "blows up" when the difference between our notions of the costs and benefits of any given action are small. Chinese menus are tough because so many items are nearly identical. Our struggles with ordering from menus illustrate well the nuances of uncertainty. I haven't eaten at McDonald's in a while, but I don't remember great mental turmoil choosing a Big Mac over a Quarter Pounder with cheese. Although the cost and benefits are nearly identical, the impact is very low. But my brain disassembles when trying to choose an appetizer at Chez Panisse. There is a finite chance that this could be the most wonderful thing I will ever eat and I don't want to miss that opportunity.

As for insects, they may not think but they certainly make
lots of decisions. What we perceive as behavior is really
just a seamless string of decisions: should I mate with you?,
should I vomit here?, should I fly off this overcrowded
rotting peach on the chance I'll find a lovely uninhabited
rotting peach? Flies make decisions forcefully, uninhibited
by memory and nostalgia. Little six-legged Fortinbras. We
like Hamlet better, because his uncertainty cuts so close to
the source of our humanity. We cannot tabulate costs and
benefits without being helplessly swayed by our memories
and emotions. We get all bollixed up with uncertainty
because we really don't see things clearly. Our minds drift
and we can't quite manage to pull the trigger. Not like
Arnold the Terminator's "*Hasta la vista*, baby." Soldiers, the
humans specifically trained to face the most wrenching of all
decisions, must learn to act with the emotionless certainty of
flies and robots.

My friend was not responding directly to Holub's
poem—I'd asked him only for his thoughts on uncertainty in general, given his research—but his inadvertent
gloss on its contents points straight to the source of this
poem's rhetorical power. By keeping his vision on the fly
at its center, Holub presents the human dimension of the
scene the more bitterly. Detachment clears the air much as
very cold temperatures can, and what is left unmentioned
in that landscape shouts back from past the poem's edge.
And that the human suffering and grief of that battlefield
is left unmentioned is one aspect of how uncertainty (and
its sometimes couching in hiddenness) inhabits all poems,

woven into their fabric in a way that is virtually structurally required. If a work is the interweaving of complex and multiple parts, it must be held by its places of openness as much as by its points of connection. Inside what is not spoken or named, some large part of a poem's work takes place—completed not on the page, but inside the writer's or reader's own fullness of being and compassion. Words on the page neither ponder nor grieve—what lives in a poem lives in us.

What I have been saying here at such great length is rather simple: to be human is to be unsure, and if the purpose of poetry is to deepen the humanness in us, poetry will be unsure as well. By multifaceted statement, by subtle resolutions and non-resolutions of circumstance and sound, by the navigation of open-ended yet resonant conclusions, good poetry helps us be more richly uncertain, in more profound ways. St. Augustine said of time, "What then is Time? If no one asks me, I know what it is. If I wish to explain it to him who asks, I do not know." The more I've thought about uncertainty in poems, the more I've come to appreciate his words. But the truth is, we don't need to understand uncertainty or time for them to accomplish their work in our lives, or in poems—all we need do is live them out and through, and that, well, that can scarcely be avoided.

CHAPTER SIX

Close Reading: Windows

Many good poems have a kind of window-moment in them—they change their direction of gaze in a way that suddenly opens a broadened landscape of meaning and feeling. Encountering such a moment, the reader breathes in some new infusion, as steeply perceptible as any physical window's increase of light, scent, sound, or air. The gesture is one of lifting, unlatching, releasing; mind and attention swing open to new-peeled vistas.

Not every good poem has a window, and it may be useful to begin by looking at one that does not, Leonard Nathan's "Falling":

FALLING

Wherever you choose to stand in this world,
that place, firm as it feels,
is a place for falling.

In my own house I fell. A dark thing,
forgotten, struck my ankle
and I fell.

Some falls are so slow, you don't know
you're falling till years later. And may be
falling still.

Leonard Nathan

This poem, written by the poet in his eighth decade, allows no escape for the reader's gaze. Its experience, echoed in each stanza's shortening line lengths, is one of tightening, narrowing, and compression. It enlarges in the way stepping off a precipice might: catharsis comes less from release into wideness than capitulation to an inescapable fate. The poem's effect is like that of looking into the polished granite of Maya Lin's Vietnam War Memorial Wall, which presents loss as historical fact—unchangeable as stone, beyond opinion—and then places upon and within that tally one's own reflection. Refusal to flinch before gravity and time, in both poem and wall, brings its own paradoxical consolations: full presence, agreement, and witness.

A "window" offers a different kind of plunging, the swerve into some new possibility of mind. The poem stops to look elsewhere, drawing on something outside its self-constructed domain and walls, whether carpentered from the conceptual, imagistic, or linguistic. A window can be held by a change of sense realms or a switch of rhetorical strategy, framed in a turn of grammar or ethical stance, sawn open by overt statement or slipped in almost unseen. Whether large or small, what I am calling a window can be recognized primarily by the experience of expansion it brings: the poem's nature is changed because its scope has become larger.

Oddly often, the device is accompanied by the image for which I've named it. One example is Philip Larkin's "High Windows"—a work in which the poet, meditating with some bitterness on changing social mores, suddenly turns to look out the physical windows from which he has taken his title:

HIGH WINDOWS

When I see a couple of kids
And guess he's fucking her and she's
Taking pills or wearing a diaphragm,
I know this is paradise

Everyone old has dreamed of all their lives—
Bonds and gestures pushed to one side

Like an outdated combine harvester,
And everyone young going down the long slide

To happiness, endlessly. I wonder if
Anyone looked at me, forty years back,
And thought, That'll be the life;
No God any more, or sweating in the dark

About hell and that, or having to hide
What you think of the priest. He
And his lot will all go down the long slide
Like free bloody birds. *And immediately*

Rather than words comes the thought of high windows:
The sun-comprehending glass,
And beyond it, the deep blue air, that shows
Nothing, and is nowhere, and is endless.

Philip Larkin

This is surely one of the stranger epiphanies of modern poetry. The mind veers from obsessive internal invective into an uninhabited, exterior image as if it has suddenly heard enough of its own voice and broken off mid-thought. The rhyme scheme's loose tether holds, but the last stanza goes, literally and figuratively, *elsewhere,* in a Hegelian—Houdiniesque?—urge to escape into a landscape devoid of connection, whether sexual, spiritual, or animal. There are no kids walking hip to hip down the street, no long slides, no birds, bloody or exultant, in Larkin's finally empty sky. The deflection can be read as a leap into some largeness beyond human dilemma or as something closer to absolution by erasure—I have read this poem, depending on my own state of spirits, both ways. Within either understanding, the closing image casts the poem into a light and scale sharply altered: the mind freed of relation falls silent.

.

Another poem in which a windowing moment occurs within its literal counterpart is Donald Justice's sonnet "The Pupil":

THE PUPIL

Picture me, the shy pupil at the door,
One small, tight fist clutching the dread Czerny.
Back then time was still harmony, not money,
And I could spend a whole week practicing for
That moment on the threshold.
                              Then to take courage,

And enter, and pass among mysterious scents,
And sit quite straight, and with a frail confidence
Assault the keyboard with a childish flourish!

Only to lose my place, or forget the key,
And almost doubt the very metronome
(Outside, the traffic, the laborers going home),

And still to bear on across Chopin or Brahms,
Stupid and wild with love equally for the storms
of C# and the calms of C.

Donald Justice

The window here is not the poem's destination, nor its main point. This sonnet's major claim-stake on the attention is its acutely felt portrait of a young person's entrance into art and art's intentions. Another of its pleasures is the elasticity with which it inhabits its form and rhyme scheme, echoing the elasticity with which a piece of music, in the hands of one who has mastered it, will be imprinted with that player's touch and no other. Still, reading it, I am always struck by the odd force of the one, seemingly casual line in which the poem steps out of its central focus and into the world of others: "(Outside, the traffic, the laborers going home)."

The observation is held in and framed by parentheses, and, in poetry, the typographical impulse to recognize a thought as extraneous quite often means that it is, and should be deleted. Yet here the poem would be sharply diminished without its conscious acknowledgment of all that lies beyond its own room. The inclusion of traffic and labor remind that art-making is luxury, not birthright. Many are tired. Many listen only to the grinding sounds of truck engines and the C# of bus brakes. The inclusion of this line reminds the reader of the cost at which the boy's search for beauty—and, by extension, the adult poet's life—have been won. An earlier thought foreshadows the theme: "Back then, time was still harmony, not money." The poem engages our relationship to beauty, but also to what is not beauty, in a life and in art—fear, hope, failure, the child-baffling mysteries of sex, our relationship to the metronome, to economics, to obligation. The pupil in the poem awakens to both text and windowed subtext, C# and C living side by side on the keys.

.

Sometimes a poem's window-opening can be so small as to be almost invisible, yet the chill air pours unmistakably through. A single word can be as consequential to a poem's ultimate experience and meaning as a single link is to the integrity of a chain. This happens in Emily Dickinson's "We grow accustomed to the Dark—," in which a series of small readjustments and transitions of mind lead the reader to the point of vertiginous plunge.

4 1 9

We grow accustomed to the Dark—
When light is put away—
As when the Neighbor holds the Lamp
To witness her Goodbye—

A Moment—We uncertain step
For newness of the night—
Then—fit our Vision to the Dark—
And meet the Road—erect—

And so of larger—Darkness—
Those Evenings of the Brain—
When not a Moon disclose a sign—
Or Star—come out—within—

The Bravest—grope a little—
And sometimes hit a Tree
Directly in the Forehead—
But as they learn to see—

Either the Darkness alters—
Or something in the sight
Adjusts itself to Midnight—
And Life steps almost straight.

Emily Dickinson

To feel the difference between other kinds of poetic transition and what I am calling a window, it may be useful to read this poem closely, noticing how each of its elements informs, revises, and charges the experience it orchestrates in mind, metabolism, and heart. We recognize a poetic window by its distinctive, precipitous feel as much as by any recognized shift of logic or ground, whereas "transition" covers all of a poem's orchestrations of altered attention, large or small. These various forms of verbal unfolding are the materials, stresses and counter-stresses, expansions, continuations, and alterations by which art's, and a life's, structures and comprehensions are made. To name them requires an almost seismographic alertness of attention;

their use, though, comes naturally. In this, we are like the character in Molière's *Le Bourgeois Gentilhomme,* surprised to learn he has been speaking prose all his life. Still, for a working writer or craft-alert reader, the exercise of making this kind of rhetorical awareness conscious, two or three times in a life, opens a new relationship to the ways in which experience lives inside creative language. It leaves in the tool chest a shining array of liftable, possible instruments for altering the angle of the seeing and feeling self.

This poem begins as many of Dickinson's do, with a general proposition: "We grow accustomed to the Dark— / When light is put away—." Next comes a simile, "As when the Neighbor holds the Lamp / To witness her Goodbye—." The line takes the opening abstraction and earths it in particular situation and image: that of stepping from a house into darkness. Because it is a neighbor's door, and not one's own, the reader feels on physically unfamiliar ground, and we enter into a subtly signaled inner displacement.

Disequilibrium is in the sound as well—"away" is a dissonant chiming of "goodbye." Dickinson's apparently native aversion to keeping her music overly neat was also actively chosen—some of her work proves her entirely capable of perfect rhyme. Incisiveness, her poems seem to say, is not the same as keeping things tidy, and insight is not achieved by domestication. Then there is the lamp's "witness"—an act of personification that makes of light something explicitly active, social—that the speaker then leaves behind. Light is expansive, inclusive of others, and life; night is solitude, the unknowable, and death. A person is rightly sent into the dark with an offered blessing.

The second stanza continues the narrative the first created. It works to consolidate the physical realm and make more fully real, and felt, the springboard image from which the poem's leap elsewhere will be made. That we are inside the grammar of simile has by now been forgotten: the reader feels her own feet testing unseen ground, feels his own body come into a surer erectness and stride once vision adjusts. We are unbalanced only momentarily, then lulled. The night is only "new"; it seems a manageable darkness. But the poem's music signals different news, forestalling easy closure. "Erect" is the least audible rhyme of the poem, falling somewhere between the first line's "step" and the second's "night."

"And so of larger—Darkness— / Those Evenings of the Brain— / When not a Moon disclose a sign— / Or Star— come out—within—": with these lines, Dickinson moves into changed terrain. The transition occurs by *fiat,* in the words "And so." The situation is altered, that is, because the poet declares it so. And even before we have read the phrase that names this increased darkening as "Evenings of the Brain," the word "larger" hints that the poet's true subject is about to emerge. (This odd, yet intuitively recognizable logic in which interior life is vaster than the outer, physical world appears as well at the start of one of Dickinson's best-known poems: "The Brain—is wider than the Sky— / for—put them side by side / The one the other will contain / With ease—and You—beside.")

The poem's landscape is no longer one of neighbors and night but of the psyche's depths, and so we find ourselves looking through the poem's first window-moment: not outward in this case, but inward. The meter has changed as well: the stanza speeds a little, moving from the previous alteration between tetrameter and trimeter into the purely three-beat lines that will be the poem's gait for its remaining stanzas.

Transformation of outer situation into an internal, metaphysical condition that is then further described again in physical terms: the pattern runs so deep in Dickinson that it could be called part of her poetry's genetic code. Everything is both general ("a Moon," a "Star," "a Tree") and sharply specific, both abstracted and drawn from the real. Dickinson's idiosyncratic capitalization raises for her figurative images some of the affection we bring to children's book characters. Yet the things being said more often than not raise terrors knowable only by the fully grown. We go to certain good poems as children go to certain stories, to be rightly frightened.

The third stanza unfolds a series of extensions that clarify, embody, and expand its introduced images. "Larger—Darkness" is revealed as "Evenings of the Brain." Those abstracted evenings are then made more actual by being emplaced in the grammar of time, with the word "When." Even the unfurnished moon and star work toward actualization: in the imagination's rhetoric, what is named absent is also present, because it has been, by naming, summoned to mind.

The further this poem travels into the psyche's interior, the more physical its describing becomes. The fourth stanza is in one way conceptually simple—the narrative simply continues into a particularly striking illustration.

But the transition works in much the way a change of key in music might: the poem moves here from subjective "we" into the more objective voice of third person plural: "The Bravest—grope a little—." This grammatical stepping back into a more objective detachment works in the psyche as physical sight works in the world. The shift invites objective wisdom into the poem: with distance, perspective increases.

The fourth stanza's image of forehead hitting tree is the poem's most vivid—and yet, if you read the poem without these lines, its larger meaning does not change. Calamity in a life (we are still in the realm of metaphor, and sense what such an image must stand for) does not of itself teach us to see, it merely embodies the penalties of darkness, the perils of blindness. What allows us to see is introduced by "But." The conjunction is a word worth stopping a moment to ponder. "But," used in the way it is here, signals changed knowledge. Its seemingly small demurral tells us that whatever it is we thought before may well be true, but it is incomplete. We must—and, in a moment, will—think again, more fully. This poem's particular "But" introduces a complex and multiple truth. A person must be willing to venture into the dark, if he or she is to learn to see there. Actual night-seeing, though, arrives only in one of two ways: either outer circumstances must relent or the eyes and self must accommodate to an irremediable "Midnight."

And what of the music in this passage of the poem? "Tree" and "see" are the only full rhymes of the poem to appear in the expected position, and that solidity contributes to the image's impact. Yet there is also enjambment—the grammar carries over between two lines and two stanzas—which causes us to hear the rhyme more lightly than we otherwise might. It also causes the poem once again to quicken, as if it were stretching toward the broadened comprehension promised by "But." That already charged conjunction is further emphasized by meter: both "But" and "Either" start their respective lines with trochee's strong downbeat, rather than the poem's more usual iambs.

I have called the third stanza the poem's first window, but for me, the true window in Dickinson's poem is contained in one word: its quick, penultimate, slipped-in "almost." The effect is so disguised it feels more truly trapdoor than window: "And Life steps almost straight." On this close-to-weightless "almost," the poem's assurance stumbles, catches. Its two syllables carry the knowledge that there are events in our lives from which no recovery is possible.

In the end, Dickinson's human news here and that of Leonard Nathan's "Falling" are drawn by different buckets from the same well—each holds the devastation of human vulnerability in a way that permits its acceptance. In "Falling," though, vulnerability is the explicit and undiluted message. Dickinson slips her abyss into a single, scarcely noticeable qualification, inside an overt statement of continuance. The difference is what makes the one poem windowless, the other windowed.

☙

All writing holds such transitions, expansions, reversals, and alterations. Between the first word of a sentence and the second, a tiny expectation rises in its listener, requiring fulfillment. An article leans toward its noun, a noun toward its verb; a preposition tells us the mind is about to be moved in time or place. Any statement made in the context of literature leaves us wondering why it was made, where it will lead; images and stories function as small, planted seeds. A poem's transitions, especially, pitch thought forward, sometimes explicitly, sometimes by verbally unsignaled changes of attention or image that simply happen, as a jump cut does in film. A window, then, will always be in some way a transition; but a transition specific in effect, a place where something in the poem not only alters but breaks different ground. As with Dickinson's poem, a window can coincide with the poem's emotional center of gravity and pivot, but as with Donald Justice's poem, it need not. It will, however, be something more than the next step forward. A window will enlarge both room and view.

Wisława Szymborska, the 1996 Nobel laureate in poetry, is a poet not much given to lifting the sash or turning the casement's handle—but here is a poem in which that happens, in this case inside a subtle switch of grammar:

SOME PEOPLE

Some people flee some other people.
In some country under a sun
and some clouds.

They abandon something close to all they've got,
sown fields, some chickens, dogs,
mirrors in which fire now preens.

Their shoulders bear pitchers and bundles.
The emptier they get, the heavier they grow.
What happens quietly: someone's dropping from exhaustion.
What happens loudly: someone's bread is ripped away,
someone tries to shake a limp child back to life.

Always another wrong road ahead of them,
always another wrong bridge
across an oddly reddish river.
Around them, some gunshots, now nearer, now farther away,
above them a plane seems to circle.

Some invisibility would come in handy,
some grayish stoniness,
or, better yet, some nonexistence
for a shorter or a longer while.

Something else will happen, only where and what.
Someone will come at them, only when and who,
in how many shapes, with what intentions.
If he has a choice,
maybe he won't be the enemy
and will leave them to some sort of life.

Wisława Szymborska

tr. by Clare Cavanaugh and Stanisław Barańczak

Szymborska's work exemplifies Chekhov's craft advice to his brother: "If you want to move your reader, write more coldly." In this she is not unlike Elizabeth Bishop or Philip Larkin, fellow practitioners of the school of chilled verse. It bears explicit noting that surface coldness, when it appears in what is also good poetry, almost invariably is drawn over something unbearable—whether heat, grief, hope, or despair. Restraint serves as protective carapace, a bulwark against reduction to pure weeping or rage. The underlying emotion is not invisible or abandoned—we see it as we might see a corpse beneath a sheet. A writer of heat (Neruda, Whitman, or Plath, for example) gives passion outright, as outcry; such poets are partisans, choosing— or forced—to speak from inside a war zone's uncalibrating tongue. Szymborska, who lived through the Second World War and the long aftermath of Soviet occupation, is no less fully present, no less fully feeling, but developed, perhaps as survival strategy, a scientist's acute observation and precise description. Her words' outer coolness is the coolness of hard data gathered in answer to harder life. In the temperature-calibration of Wisława Szymborska's writing, Dickinson's "almost" is close to boiling. Yet no alert reader could mistake Szymborska for a person free of strong feeling.

The window-moment in this poem is a mirror reversal of the one in Donald Justice's sonnet. In "The Pupil," everything is personal, the lens of vision held close, until our attention is brought by one quick swerve to the world of others. In "Some People," the lens's vision is kept almost entirely long, the description placed into the general. This distancing in itself grieves, given what is being described. We recognize the subtractive voice: here is newsreel knowledge, the journalist's indecently abbreviated glance into the tragedies of strangers. It presents the dehumanization of mass crises, individual fates surrendered to the language of "collateral damage" and recited numbers. The poem, though, is not without its abrading details—the chickens, the lifted-up body of the child. When fire "preens" in a mirror, in one kind of language choice, when invisibility would "come in handy," in another, the reader's alertness cannot help but rise to the poem's own. Even those who read Szymborska in translation can safely trust: this is not the language of stupefaction.

In the final lines, however, generalization lifts, and in that moment Szymborska shows both horror's blindfold and its removal:

Something else will happen, only where and what.
Someone will come at them, only when and who,
in how many shapes, with what intentions.
If he has a choice,
maybe he won't be the enemy
and will leave them to some sort of life.

"*If he has a choice.*" With that line's grammatical knife twist, certain kinds of awareness we were not even aware had been suppressed rush back into the poem. Individuality enters. The reminder enters that war and its violence are acts of personal responsibility, personal choice. The slenderest blade edge of hope enters. Do not hope for too much, the reader is cautioned—the last line returns to both bleakness and generalization. Still, with that small pronoun "he," human agency returns: the bedrock decision to harm or not harm rests always in individual hands, and cannot be disguised as something generic or collective. The window here (as in Donald Justice's sonnet) alters the poem's relationship to its moral dimension. It brings that realm, quite simply, into explicit and recognizable view. The British philosopher Stuart Hampshire has suggested, in *Innocence and Experience,* that a culture's moral sensibility depends less on divisions between "moral" or "immoral" than on whether any particular issue—slavery, opprobrium regarding sexual preference and practices, certain uses of power—is perceived as falling within the realm of morality at all. He offers, that is, the view that morality in our lives is a function of looking through a particular window. The awakening of an unsentimental and yet fully compassionate judgment in this and other of Wisława Szymborska's poems is often set in motion by exactly this kind of shifting in and out of a morally based stance. That this happens almost entirely below awareness, accomplished by quick and close to invisible sleights of hand, is what marks this the work of a poet, not a jurist.

.

To remind us of the existence of others when we have fallen into the maze of interior, subjective life is one large part of the work of literature's windows. They keep us from stifling solipsism, by returning the personal self to connection with what is beyond it. They lead us back toward some sense of the whole. In *King Lear*'s third act, such a window clearly opens. Lear, Kent, and the Fool stand on the heath. First Lear addresses the storm, which he cannot keep separate for more than a moment from his self-created subjective condition:

> *Rumble thy bellyful! Spit, fire! spout, rain!*
> *Nor rain, wind, thunder, fire, are my daughters:*
> *I tax not you, you elements with unkindness;*
> *I never gave you kingdom, call'd you children;*
> *You owe me no subscription; then let fall*
> *Your horrible pleasure; here I stand, your slave,*
> *A poor infirm, weak, and despis'd old man:—*
> *But yet I call you servile ministers,*
> *That will with two pernicious daughters join*
> *Your high-engender'd battles against a head*
> *So old and white as this. O! O! 'tis foul!*

Soon after, standing outside the door of a hovel, Lear refuses to join the others in its shelter, saying the tempest's blows buffer even more painful thought. He then goes on:

> *Poor naked wretches, whereso'er you are,*
> *That bide the pelting of this pitiless storm,*
> *How shall your houseless heads and unfed sides,*
> *Your loop'd and window'd raggedness, defend*
> *From seasons such as these? O, I have ta'en*
> *Too little care of this! Take physic, pomp;*
> *Expose thyself to feel what wretches feel . . .*

This recognition of the larger tasks of a king—the care of those of his subjects who are homeless, ill-clothed, and hungry—is a moment's sanity, releasing Lear from his entrancement in self. The storm becomes externally real when the suffering of others is felt also as real, and vice versa. We who watch and listen also come for this moment to our larger senses, before plunging back into the tragedy's inexorable course. We are reminded that Lear's deafness to the depth behind Cordelia's first, mild words is part of a more extensive narrowing of heart and vision, whose only cure is openness to exposure. In Shakespeare, abdication of rule and the failure to love are not different: both are shown as evasions needing correction.

·

The use of windows is not confined to poetry. They appear in prose as well, sometimes at the level of sentence or paragraph, sometimes in scene or chapter. Here is an example from Don DeLillo's *Underworld,* especially visible in an archived preliminary draft of the novel's opening in which the final paragraph breaks haven't yet been put into place:

> He speaks in your voice, American, and there's a shine in his eye that's halfway hopeful. It's a school day, sure, but he's nowhere near the classroom. He wants to be here instead, standing in the shadow of this old rust-hulk of a structure, and it's hard to blame him—this metropolis of steel and concrete and flaky paint and cropped grass and enormous Chesterfield packs aslant on the scoreboards, a couple of

cigarettes jutting from each. Longing on a large scale is what makes history.

The window effect of the last sentence given here is immediate and profound. DeLillo's momentary shift from the particular to the abstract opens the book's voice to speak from a larger perspective, and to move from the individual boy to the larger cultural exploration which will be the book's focus. The narration reflects this change clearly as it goes on:

Longing on a large scale is what makes history. This is just a kid with a local yearning but he is part of an assembling crowd, anonymous thousands off the buses and trains, people in narrow columns tramping over the swing bridge above the river, and even if they are not a migration or a revolution, some vast shaking of the soul, they bring with them the body heat of a great city and their own small reveries and desperations, the unseen something that haunts the day—men in fedoras and sailors on shore leave, the stray tumble of their thoughts, going to a game.

Many of the chapters in Melville's *Moby-Dick* can also be seen to function as windows, some looking into the sea, the ship, or the bodies of whales, others facing outward. One chapter, for example, lists all known paintings and images of whales, beginning with those in books and above pub doors, ending with whale silhouettes found in mountain ridge lines and whale shapes traceable among the stars. These departures from the central story throw Ahab's revenge-quest and constriction into sharp relief; they remind that what he cannot rejoin—cannot even perceive—is a world infinite, playful, various, and open without limits. Virginia Woolf's *To the Lighthouse* is multiply windowed in the "Time Passes" section alluded to in the last chapter. Time appears in falling plaster and loosening fabric; a marriage or death is telegraphed in a bracket-held sentence; the war's distant, thudding artillery trembles glass tumblers inside a cupboard. This last image shows one of windowing's particular capacities: to reverse figure and ground, letting the large be known by its effect on the small. This of course is not only a literary device—it is how we know life itself. Longing on a large scale makes history, which wears a fedora in one decade, a baseball cap in another.

.

Two British poems of the Second World War, Keith Douglas's "How to Kill" and Henry Reed's "Naming of Parts," draw hard on the power of windows in similar ways. Each forces the eyes toward its subject more strongly by turning them also away. That oscillation of view may be the only way these poems could have been written, or be read, at all. Experience can only be lived through, yet its full brunt is often something we try to avoid. We distract ourselves, grow sleepy, obsess on one thing in order not to look at another. Art is a way to make experience unavoidable, not least by acts of stepping back in ways whose end effect is the collapse of distance. The looking elsewhere of these two poems is not evasion, not an armoring against presence. It is, like the heath scene in *King Lear*, the aperture through which exposure deepens.

Henry Reed's "Naming of Parts" is the opening poem in a five-part series, "Lessons of the War."

NAMING OF PARTS

To-day we have naming of parts. Yesterday,
We had daily cleaning. And to-morrow morning,
We shall have what to do after firing. But to-day,
To-day we have naming of parts. Japonica
Glistens like coral in all of the neighboring gardens,

And to-day we have naming of parts.
This is the lower sling swivel. And this
Is the upper sling swivel, whose use you will see,
When you are given your slings. And this is the piling swivel,
Which in your case you have not got. The branches
Hold in the gardens their silent, eloquent gestures,

Which in our case we have not got.
This is the safety-catch, which is always released
With an easy flick of the thumb. And please do not let me
See anyone using his finger. You can do it quite easy
If you have any strength in your thumb. The blossoms
Are fragile and motionless, never letting anyone see

Any of them using their finger.
And this you can see is the bolt. The purpose of this

Is to open the breech, as you see. We can slide it
Rapidly backwards and forwards: we call this
Easing the spring. And rapidly backwards and forwards
The early bees are assaulting and fumbling the flowers:

They call it easing the Spring.
They call it easing the Spring: it is perfectly easy
If you have any strength in your thumb: like the bolt,
And the breech, and the cocking-piece, and the point of balance,
Which in our case we have not got; and the almond-blossom
Silent in all of the gardens and the bees going backwards and forwards,
For to-day we have naming of parts.

Henry Reed

Japonica blossoms, bees, the flowering almond, the meaning-doubled Spring—each breaks the poem from the mechanical death spell it chants. The fragrant surround releases the mind as if from a nightmare not acknowledged as nightmare, into an alternative version of what is possible: fumbling assaults undertaken for sweetness. The twice-named silence of the poem's trees may not be judgment, but it is measure: each time the mind moves from weapon to garden, from garden to weapon, we are reminded that the exchange of one for the other remains a choice.

There is another fissure in this poem as well, found within the hiddenness-device of an absence. The reader can't help but notice the one rifle part the poem does fail to name. It is skipped over somewhere inside the phrase "To-morrow morning, we shall have what to do after firing."

A good test for the effect of a poem's window-moments is to see what the poem is like without them. If read without its natural-world images, "Naming of Parts" can still turn on its ironies, on "the point of balance, / Which in our case we have not got." But the almost unbearable grief-sense is oddly reduced if the poem is stripped of its other, counterbalancing world, the one in which our human wars and fears hold no meaning or weight.

"How to Kill" is one of the most harrowing of a century of harrowing poems.

HOW TO KILL

Under the parabola of a ball,
a child turning into a man,
I looked into the air too long.
The ball fell in my hand, it sang
in the closed fist: Open Open
Behold a gift designed to kill.

Now in my dial of glass appears
the soldier who is going to die.
He smiles, and moves about in ways
his mother knows, habits of his.
The wires touch his face: I cry
NOW. Death, like a familiar, hears

and look, has made a man of dust
of a man of flesh. This sorcery

I do. Being damned, I am amused
to see the centre of love diffused
and the wave of love travel into vacancy.
How easy it is to make a ghost.

The weightless mosquito touches
her tiny shadow on the stone,
and with how like, how infinite
a lightness, man and shadow meet.
They fuse. A shadow is a man
when the mosquito death approaches.

Keith Douglas

Keith Douglas died in the war, at age twenty-four. The blow of his poem's conveyed knowledge is precisely what the drillmaster of "Naming of Parts" attempts to forestall: the man is not supposed to be present on the battlefield, only the instrument-soldier whose tasks have been rehearsed to the point of automation. Douglas's windows—and this is a poem made almost entirely of glass lights and wooden muntin dividers—keep bringing humanness back into the realm of the visible. The opening image of childhood throws a light that erases all distance between the speaker and the soldier he kills. Both are flesh, not implement; both are still boys. "He smiles, and moves about in ways / his mother knows, habits of his" is a sentence almost unbearable to read. It forces the gaze from battlefield anonymity into the roundness of life. The poem as a whole, for me, is almost unbearable to read. It is too fully conscious.

It requires its reader to enter also into a state of damnation, recognizing our own failure in, and responsibility for, what it describes. And, with the same effect as in "Naming of Parts," this poem shifts the eyes to the natural world's coinhabitance of each of our moments, its alternate possibilities traveling alongside our own. Here, though, even the insect world is swept in: the mosquito becomes part of the total eclipse and obliteration that is war-death. In the end, the poem itself stands as the only testament to what war has taken.

Every poem—every work of art—is already working, when considered as a whole, as a kind of window: art is a way to release our attention from immediacy's grip into gestures that encompass, draw from, and remind of more expansive constellations and connection. The experience of an enlarged intimacy is not the only reason to want art in our lives, but it is a central reason. The windows that break open the boundaries of a poem, piece of music, or painting do the same work: they awaken and give entrance to what might otherwise not be recognized, felt, or known as inseparably part of the story. Sometimes this is awareness of the moral realm, sometimes awareness that our fate is without perimeter, joined with the fate of others. Sometimes it is the recognition of our human vulnerability, sometimes of the replenishing housed outside the human. Sometimes the changed awareness is simply the knowledge that a different relationship to experience might be possible. Art's request and command is that we know our lives in their specificity but also in their wholeness and vastness. Wherever the gaze rests, art will draw it also elsewhere, will remind that there is always *more*. Alice does not stop and face her own reflection in the looking-glass: she travels through it.

Good writing will have points of view—but they will be plural. No truly good work of literature faces in only one direction, is single in its allegiances, or looks at existence from only one angle, one theory. Theory—including literary theory—is the stance of argument, not of art. To live only in the socioeconomic self is to starve the self of its capacity for purposeless joy. To live only in the ideological is to deny ourselves uncertainty, fragility, loss. To live only in the emotional and autobiographical is to ignore what transcends the personal story and ego. To live only in the intellect or narrowly spiritual is to miss the saturation of the senses. Let us close then with Czesław Miłosz's "Winter," a poem which turns toward almost every direction of human life, whose fidelity is, in the end, simply to life—and whose midpoint turn to the vocative "you" is, I believe, among the most breathtaking transitions and window-openings to be found anywhere in literature, in its intimacy and in what it summons.

WINTER

The pungent smells of a California winter,
Grayness and rosiness, an almost transparent full moon.
I add logs to the fire, I drink and I ponder.

"In Ilawa," the news item said, "at age 70
Died Aleksander Rymkiewicz, poet."

He was the youngest in our group, I patronized him slightly,
Just as I patronized others for their inferior minds
Though they had many virtues I couldn't touch.

And so I am here, approaching the end
Of the century and of my life. Proud of my strength
Yet embarrassed by the clearness of the view.

Avant-gardes mixed with blood.
The ashes of inconceivable arts.
An omnium-gatherum of chaos.

I passed judgment on that. Though marked myself.
This hasn't been the age for the righteous and the decent.
I know what it means to beget monsters
And to recognize in them myself.

You, moon, You, Aleksander, fire of cedar logs.
Waters close over us, a name lasts but an instant.
Not important whether the generations hold us in memory.
Great was that chase with the hounds for the unattainable meaning of
    the world.

And now I am ready to keep running
When the sun rises beyond the borderlands of death.
I already see mountain ridges in the heavenly forest
Where, beyond every essence, a new essence waits.

You, music of my late years, I am called
by a sound and a color which are more and more perfect.

Do not die out, fire. Enter my dreams, love.
Be young forever, seasons of the earth.

Czesław Miłosz

tr. by Czesław Miłosz and Robert Hass

CHAPTER SEVEN

Poetry and the Constellation of Surprise

Art's brightness is a strangely untarnishing silver. One of the distinguishing powers of great art is its capacity to unseal its own experience not once, but many times. A Beethoven quartet many times heard, a painting by Bonnard looked at for decades, does not lose the ability to lift us out of one way of being and knowing and emplace us, altered, into another. A poem long memorized can raise in its holder, mid-saying, stunned tears. Pound described the paradox simply: "Poetry is news that stays news." Why this is so, and how it is done, has something to do with the way good art preserves its own capacity to surprise.

The anonymous "Western Wind," one of the oldest poems in English literature, provides a good starting point for investigating perennial newness:

Western wind, when wilt thou blow?
The small rain down can rain.

Christ, that my love were in my arms,
And I in my bed again.

The poem is a small and intimate crisis, preserved intact through time by memorable sounds and by its expansion of the perimeters of existence in every direction: vertical and horizontal; interior and outward; emotional and spiritual. Its images cut through both familiarity and complacency. They are blades that feel freshly sharpened each time they are read.

Other conceptual realms are not like this. Even discoveries as revolutionary as those made by Copernicus, Kepler, and Newton are soon taken for granted. Impersonal, emotionally neutral, our comprehension of solar system or gravity is as calmly fixed in the mental landscape as a long-familiar chair or backyard rock. Science's discoveries may—and do—raise wonder, but their usefulness does not depend on our astonishment at their existence. In art, though, this moment's human response *is* the discovery. A work of art is not color knifed or brushed onto a canvas, not shaped rock or fired clay, a vibrating cello string, black ink on a page—it is our participatory, agile, and responsive collaboration with those forms, colors, symbols, and sounds.

We write or read poems because we need them. The first poems were work songs, love songs, war songs, lullabies, prayers—rituals meant to carry assistance. "Western Wind" carries in its lines primordial dilemma, primordial longing: here is a person far out to sea in terms of geography, weather, and condition of soul. A literal bewilderment holds the music of the first line, whose sounded "w" runs through each of the most basic English-language words of questioning: "what," "where," "why," "when," "how," "who." We hear also the open and permeable "O" of the line's end word, an "o" we must commit ourselves to with the full breath in order to say at all. And we hear the narrower vowels the line must pass through before it, and the study in "a" sounds that follows. This poem's music builds a suspension bridge between asking and answer.

The nameless poet speaks in the intimate grammatical voice of prayer and direct address. Yet his I/Thou isn't turned to the divine, it is spoken to wind; the word "Christ" appears almost in passing, in a tone half prayer-invocation, half curse. The poem's third line summons, in the course of eight words, spiritual life, erotic life, and their connection within the intensities of human longing. And then the last line arrives, which both sustains the poem's emergency—the line is held in the grammar of wishing, not having—and resolves it without resolving, by tucking us safely into the longed-for bed with the rhyme-promise of "again" and "rain." One must surely follow the other, the poem's sound-murmur assures, though the rational mind knows well they need not. Even the rain itself may or may not come. In this way of multiplicity and music, poetry instructs in the navigation of essentially unnavigable circumstances and truths. We are going to die; we live now. We are solitary; we are connected to the beloved, to weather, to (perhaps) the divine. We despair; we hope. This quatrain's mitered joining of the unresolvable and beauty crafts a vessel sturdy enough to have crossed a thousand years, but one also as fragile, fugitive, and significant as a puff of smoke.

Poems are like the emotions they awaken in us: not preservable object, but living event. Local and unextractable from the body, emotion is an experience that informs of current circumstance, current needs, and then disappears. "What is love, 'tis not hereafter; / Present mirth wants present laughter," sings Feste in Shakespeare's *Twelfth Night,* half courting, half warning. Even if we desire, grieve, or protest something remembered, it is this moment's desire or sorrow, this moment's anger, we feel. In the instant we cease to care, the past loses its sting.

Poetry's words can be ink- and sound-stored stably, then, but the poem itself cannot. It is the score to a music for which we are instrument and audience both, held in the procedures of its making. The "meaning" of "Western Wind"—or of any truly good poem—is like certain chemical reactions: evaporative, volatile, and elusive. Its lines waver between what is here and what is not, between what the grammar tells us of truth and the music's alternative promise. Poetic epiphany gives off a kind of protective mist; it exudes an amnesiac against general recall. The poem must be read or said through fully to be fully known. In this is perhaps the first explanation for the always-original brightness of good poems: what is impossible to remember will (re)appear as new.

What surprises, etymology tells us, is what is "beyond grasp." Even the mind of the author cannot seem to keep what has been found: great poems exceed their creators.

They are more capacious, capricious, compassionate, original, witty, strange, avaricious for beauty and range. The writer's life, the historical times, do not make the art. Art makes art. Any real creative discovery is a leap inconceivable until taken—not least, as we will see also in a later chapter, because inconceivability is part of its nature.

⤜

Cognitive and creative discoveries are made in the same way as much of biological life is: by acts of generative recombination. Disparate elements are brought together to see if they might make a viable new whole. To explore how this happens, we must begin with cognition's own beginnings, in the construction and discernment of patterns. From the infant's "buzzing and blooming confusion," in William James's phrase, we assemble a comprehensible world by perceiving first what stays, what recurs. Only after such patterns are in place can we begin to recognize departures from the template, and to see which combinations are new and might newly inform. Creative epiphany is much the same: a knowledge won against the patterns of predictable thought, feeling, or phrase.

Surprise, then, is epiphany's first flavor. It is the emotion by which we register shifted knowledge, in a poem, in a life. Good poems make self and world knowable in changed ways, bring us into an existence opened, augmented, and altered. To awaken into new circumference—as we see in stories ranging from *Alice in Wonderland* to *Gulliver's Travels*— is to be startled. (In Kafka's "The Metamorphosis," Gregor

Samsa's utter calmness inside his new form is what most unsettles the reader.) And further, surprise not only signals the recognition that something has changed, it is part of the changing.

The bigger the leap of a new connection, the more surprise it will hold. The most profound discoveries—those described as revolutionary or "earth-shaking"—are those, like the Copernican rearrangement of sun and planets, that challenge and replace our most daily perceptions and unquestioned assumptions. In science, though, as we've seen, such surprises are soon integrated into different but now settled patterns. In the realm of art, the new is not object but process, and cannot be kept pinned down in the mind.

The Latin verb *cogitare,* "to think," has at its root in the act of shaking things together, and the idea that agitation is needed to make something new is found both in myths and in social and political revolutions worldwide. The etymology of *intelligo* adds something different: intelligence involves sorting, intention, selection. This recalls Chekhov's definition of talent: the ability to tell the essential and inessential apart. The third quality of creative making's cognitive tripod is different again: counterfactual thought's recombinant question, "What if?"

"What if" resides on a spectrum—it inhabits equally the scientist's centrifuge and a child's broomstick horse, though there is a difference between them. Play shakes things up, often quite literally, in new ways. But while the results of play both instruct and bring pleasure, they rarely jolt. Make-believe has an indispensable role in early life precisely because it doesn't "count": play is exploration free of repercussion. The researcher, meanwhile, hopes an experiment's result might actually matter.

These distinctions clarify why some poems seem essential, while others, however accomplished and interesting of surface, do not. Deep surprise is the way the mind signals itself that a thing perceived or thought is consequential, that a discovery may be of genuine use. The experience itself, though, especially in responding to a work of art, may well be felt as some different emotion, the one that follows; surprise, neuroscientists report, lasts half a second at most; and so the reader may notice the powerful upsurge of grief or compassion or wonder a good poem brings, but not the surprise that released it. Surprise plays a major role in survival's own sorting—what most surprises will be most strongly acted on, and most strongly learned. The poems we carry forward, as individuals and as cultures, are those that strike us powerfully enough that they call up the need for their own recall.

·

How is it that something that lasts a half second can be so essential, not only to art but to our very survival? Not least is the particular way startlement transforms the one who is startled. Among other things, surprise magnetizes attention. An infant hearing an unexpected sound will stop and stare hard—the experience of surprise is itself surprising. It is also, literally, arresting: in a person strongly startled, the heart rate momentarily plummets. The whole being pauses, to better grasp what's there. Surprise also opens the mind, frees it from preconception. Surprise does not weigh its object as "good" or "bad"; though that may follow, its question is simply "What is it?," asked equally of any sudden change. Startlement, it seems, erases the known for the new. The facial expression of surprise, according to one researcher, is close to rapture, to the openness of a baby's first awakeness. Charles Darwin, in *The Expression of the Emotions in Man and Animals,* grouped surprise with astonishment, amazement, and wonder.

In poetry, surprise deepens, gathers, and purifies attention in the same way: the mind of preconception is stopped, to allow a more acute taking-in. A taxonomy of poetic surprise covers many levels—word, syntax, concept, image, rhetoric, any of these can present us with something unexpected. Disruption of pattern (overt or subtle) can take place in structure, rhythm, approach, meter, or rhyme. Surprise can rest entirely in a poem's textural surface or in subtext alone. The unlikely thing may be the choice of what is looked at, and one subtle path to surprise is through the movement and refocusing of attention. Certain haiku, such as Issa's "Don't worry, spider—I keep house casually," simply bring the unnoticed to notice. It is as if the walls of the room you are in were suddenly to drop away and the house next door—which, after all, you did know was there—were suddenly sitting companionably within view, except the neighbor is the spider, and the house your own.

Whether by means large or small, noticed or almost imperceptible, poetry's startlements displace the existing self with a changed one. Even the fine-grained surprise of a single line's enjambment is pause and question and revision of comprehension; as with puns, or Japanese poetry's pivot words, two conditions of mind are summoned, each of which jostles the other. Keats pointed to these almost intangible transmutations of meaning and felt experience when he wrote that poetry "surprises by fine excess." In the density of poetry's rendering of attention, the world—and so the experiencing self—takes on a surplus abundance. It offers the same pleasure we feel before a discovered spring: we know thirst will be answered unmeagerly, with a generosity far beyond its own measure.

Surprise carries an inverse relationship to that which harnesses self and will: it is the emotion of a transition not self-created. Though infants can visibly surprise themselves by sneezing, there is no self-tickling. We tend not to laugh at our own jokes, at least when alone. Yet one of the reasons a poem—or any creative effort—is undertaken is precisely to surprise yourself by what you may find. Poems appear to come from the self only to those who do not write them. The maker experiences them as gift, implausibly won from the collaboration of individual with language, self with unconscious, personal association and concept with the world's uncontrollable materials, weathers, events. Picasso said of his paintings, "I do not seek, I find."

Insight's arrival as if from outside the self has been described not only by artists but by biologists, economists, mathematicians. The early-twentieth-century mathematical prodigy Ramanujan claimed his theorems came to him from a whispering goddess. If you leave out the goddess, the description turns out to be not uncommon among mathematicians—many radically new propositions, it seems, are proven after, not en route to, their first appearance in the mind.

We are beings often skeptical of, made worried by, surprise; we are also beings who seek it out. Polynesian transoceanic explorers in hollowed-out logs, Atlantic City gamblers, and mountain climbers sleeping cliff-suspended, hung from a half-dozen hammered-in pitons, share the willingness to submit themselves to the unknown. Risk of failure—not unfamiliar to even the desk-bound—amplifies the exhilaration of success.

Surprise, as we've seen, is the gate through which the new must pass. If something in a poem startles others, it will have startled its maker first. Robert Lowell wrote (speaking in one poem about his others), "My Dolphin, you only guide me by surprise." "No surprise for the writer, no surprise for the reader," said Robert Frost.

When I began mulling over these questions, I raised the question of abiding surprise with a friend, while walking. We reached a ridge, and I said, "We've been here many times before, why is it always so new?" I myself was thinking of E. O. Wilson's theory of sight lines and African savannah; of the complex textures of sky, leaves, and grasses; of the role of cloud and mist in Chinese paintings. She answered, "Because it isn't me."

The world's beauty continually surprises in no small part because it is not controlled by self or what self knows. Even something as plain as a sand grain or pebble, considered closely, can liberate us from conscious mind's constriction, the effect of ego's dominance described earlier by Bashō:

"If we were to gain mastery over things, we would find their lives would vanish under us without a trace." A city would serve as well—say, Lorca's New York. For Whitman, a country. Release of narrow view lies behind surprise in humor, intellectual riddle, tragic catharsis—why should it not lie as well behind the perennial and fugitive beauty of the objective world, which is not of our making and does not exist for our use? Astonishment's other side is our powerlessness over the view.

Times Square, New York City

❦

Lyric epiphany is democratic, equally intimate with Aeschylus and the stand-up comic. If poetry's effects on us seem to link it more often to the former, its economy and means of meaning-making are nearer the latter. E. E. Cummings, when asked his technique in poetry, responded: "I can express it in fifteen words, by quoting the eternal question and immortal answer of burlesque: 'Would you hit a woman with a baby? No, I'd hit her with a brick.'" He went on. "Like the burlesque comedian, I am abnormally fond of that precision which creates movement." The joke's technique recalls another, from Groucho Marx: "Outside a dog, a book is a man's best friend; inside a dog, it's too dark to read." The mechanism of the gesture in both instances is sleight of hand, worked on a single word's disparate meanings. Each turns on a preposition's double reading: in the first joke, "with"; in the second, "outside." English prepositions reify relationships that are more fluid in languages that use inflection, and rigidity always opens the gate to the comic. But the lesser joke quoted by Cummings rests on slapstick's unjustified aggressions; Groucho Marx's raises a reminder of isolation and friendlessness, of the depth of a night in which a book and a dog are the only two options and even they are then stripped away. His invention holds word-wit in its right hand; in its left, the sufferings of Jonah and Job.

Familiar jokes continue to make us laugh for the same reasons that known poems continue to move and surprise. We perennially fall for what enlists us into an experience so simply and seductively offered that we cannot refuse the offered, open door. Neither a poem's nor a joke's reason for being can be found without remaking the motions of mind that create it. A joke's punch line, like a poem's meaning, is not in its words, but in what we make of them—and they of us. As with poems, our amnesia to certain jokes is almost complete; when it isn't, we sometimes laugh harder, at the inertia of our own prat-fallible mind. The performing arts—which include comedy, poetry, music, dance, and magic, as well as theater—ask of us not only the theater's well-known suspension of disbelief, but also suspension of foreknowledge. All partake of something that lies at the core of ritual: the reenactment of and entrance into a mystery that can be touched and entered but not possessed.

The more surprise in good poetry is looked at, the more poetry's work seems close to the work of the comic and trickster. Each unfastens those things we most think we know, and in humor, as in the arts and in science, it's when fundamental and unexamined assumptions of mind and nature are most shaken that we are most moved. "Wit" was once a synonym for simple "knowing." Groucho Marx's words feel close to those of a poem not only in their undertow sadness, but in that undertow's very existence, in its challenge to deep preconception. Jokes are supposed to be funny, are they not? Yet what makes a good joke good is precisely that it is not merely mechanically funny; it also shows us something both discomforting and true. We are alone. Inside a dog, and us, it is dark.

Against gravity and entropic loss, a poem proposes the levitations of fine excess and gratuitous beauty—sound-trance's memorability; the aerial devices of implication; metaphor's democratic conjugation with all existence; the praise of whatever is for what it is. In a painting, a small square of sunlight rests on the rounded shoulder of a glass vase, preserved impossibly against time's passage; the pause in a piece of music by Mozart stops the heart for no reason except that it is there. Against transience, art provides a witnessing endurance; against the stringencies of survival, it offers the moment's dalliance or chosen disappearance. The love poem born of unfulfilled desire embraces its own longing. The poem of love's fulfillment carries somewhere within it, however lightly, the shadow of time and death. A painted apple cannot be eaten. As evolution's creatures, we align with goal attainment, self-protection, and the useful. The part of art which is art, and not device, unshackles us from usefulness almost entirely. It emplaces us far into those impractical conditions that nonetheless feel to us somehow essential: laughter, contemplation, wonder, tears.

If we are to test these ideas upon poems, the recalcitrant case interests most, and so in place of more obviously strange or self-consciously new examples, I have chosen three works whose challenges to preconception both differ from one another and are not easy to name. C. P. Cavafy's "Ithaka" is as good a place as any to start—a poem that retains through many readings the power to peel the soul freshly from sleep.

ITHAKA

As you set out for Ithaka
hope your road is a long one,
full of adventure, full of discovery.
Laistrygonians, Cyclops,
angry Poseidon—don't be afraid of them:
you'll never find things like that on your way
as long as you keep your thoughts raised high,
as long as a rare excitement
stirs your spirit and your body.
Laistrygonians, Cyclops,
wild Poseidon—you won't encounter them
unless you bring them along inside your soul,
unless your soul sets them up in front of you.

Hope your road is a long one.
May there be many summer mornings when,
with what pleasure, what joy,
you enter harbors you're seeing for the first time;
may you stop at Phoenician trading stations
to buy fine things,
mother of pearl and coral, amber and ebony,
sensual perfume of every kind—
as many sensual perfumes as you can;
and may you visit many Egyptian cities
to learn and go on learning from their scholars.

Keep Ithaka always in your mind.
Arriving there is what you're destined for.

But don't hurry the journey at all.
Better if it lasts for years,
so you're old by the time you reach the island,
wealthy with all you've gained on the way,
not expecting Ithaka to make you rich.

Ithaka gave you the marvelous journey.
Without her you wouldn't have set out.
She has nothing left to give you now.

And if you find her poor, Ithaka won't have fooled you.
Wise as you will have become, so full of experience,
you'll have understood by then what these Ithakas mean.

C. P. Cavafy

tr. by Edmund Keeley and Philip Sherrard

Cavafy's stamp of mind is hermetic, not martial. The self encountering "Ithaka" knows itself readjusted—yet it is difficult to articulate quite where the transformation lies. Modest of surface, perambulative, the poem's language is plain, its tone unheated even when speaking of marvels; and though sufficient detail is given for the narrative, sensuous, and image-hungry mind to be fed, even these offerings are evocative but not detailed. Summer mornings, exotic places, mother-of-pearl, ebony, and perfume—these are semaphores for the sensory world, glittering samples flashed on a street corner to pull in a mark. On first look, the poem seems filled more with abstraction and the hypnosis of repetition than with any identifiable epiphanic revelation. "Full of adventure, full of discovery"; "with what pleasure, what joy"—such paralleled doublings with small variation are among Cavafy's most frequent constructions, and the experience they offer is one of tellings, not showings. The poem refers to monsters and adventure, yet its terrors are so mildly murmured, they pass unfelt.

But look again: "As you set out for Ithaka, hope your road is a long one." Odysseus's journey was indeed long, but its ten-year duration was not (despite the lengthy interval with Circe) Odysseus's desire. To make it so is Cavafy's additive invention. Slipped in so simply and quietly that one hardly notices what it says, or that it is the only phrase the poem repeats exactly, the statement cuts sharply against the grain. Hope of delay and long travel not only inverts our usual cultural attitude toward pursuit and goal, it unravels basic dynamics of our Metazoan animal nature. Desire, ingenuity, and effort aim, in mammalian life, toward resolution, not their own prolonging. Even this poem's relationship to its title embodies its central point: the city in Cavafy's poem is never reached.

Cavafy is like the magician whose gestures are made so far out in the open they are almost impossible to see: each time, we feel their outcome as surprise. By this smoke-and-mirror invisibility, the central imperative statement skirts both the oppressively didactic and staling. Still, if the premise is true that a poem's volatile effects on us stem from the reader's inability to hold its full meaning entirely in mind, the overt statement cannot be the sole source of "Ithaka"'s power. Nor is "Hope your road is a long one" the only triggering phrase by which I myself recall the poem. While there are other counter-wisdoms (most sharply the suggestion that all monsters are self-created), the plumb weight of the poem falls at its end. For me, the words by which this poem returns to mind are "Ithaka gave you the marvelous journey," and what follows: "And if you find her poor, Ithaka won't have fooled you. / Wise as you will have become, so full of experience, / you'll have understood by then what these Ithakas mean." The lines are a small brutality, chilling in their knocking aside of what once was desired. In this English-language translation, the feminine pronoun does its work as well. In it is the one reminder that Penelope is also by these words being dismissed, and with her all our felt, human connections to family and home.

A ritual must be passed through with the whole body, not glimpsed through a door. However efficient a poem's any single syllable may sometimes be, "Ithaka"'s entirety is needed to make its case and journey; this could not be a poem of five or seven lines. Ordinarily we think repetition must be antithetical to surprise or intensification—how can the already-known bring fresh news? Yet when a clown attempts and fails some task repeatedly, each time looking more puzzled, the audience laughs more loudly each time. Or we might think of Charlie Brown's faith that Lucy will someday hold the football in place for his kick: the motif resides in the knowledge that the betrayal has happened so many times before. Repetition allows saturation, and its particular content's meaning is not the same as a thing said or done only once. By "Ithaka"'s conclusion, the effects of recurrence and allusion have deepened the poem's revelation as long rubbing with sheep's wool and beeswax deepens the grain and color of a table while giving it shine. The experience of recognition, of seeing fully what was always there to be seen—in life, as in the poem—is as much as anything "Ithaka"'s, and poetry's, surprise.

A different purchase on surprise can be found in Seamus Heaney's "Oysters," a poem that exemplifies the close-woven attention to experience and language which, fully followed, leads to a complex liberation for the writer, for the reader.

OYSTERS

Our shells clacked on the plates.
My tongue was a filling estuary,
My palate hung with starlight:
As I tasted the salty Pleiades
Orion dipped his foot into the water.

Alive and violated,
They lay on their beds of ice:
Bivalves: the split bulb
and philandering sigh of ocean.
Millions of them ripped and shucked and scattered.

We had driven to that coast
Through flowers and limestone
And there we were, toasting friendship,

Laying down a perfect memory
In the cool of thatch and crockery.

Over the Alps, packed deep in hay and snow,
The Romans hauled their oysters south to Rome:
I saw damp panniers disgorge
The frond-lipped, brine-stung
Glut of privilege

And was angry that my trust could not repose
In the clear light, like poetry or freedom
Leaning in from the sea. I ate the day
Deliberately, that its tang
Might quicken me all into verb, pure verb.

Seamus Heaney

We stand in this poem with a master of shaking things together—the personal with the historical, the local with the large, the life of the body that eats with the life of the feeling heart and thoughtful mind. Selective intelligence manifests as well—part of this poem's specific gravity is its confident leaving out of the inessential. The resultant speed is discernible even in the first line: "Our shells clacked on the plates." We notice first the sure onomatopoeia of "clacked" against "plates." Less obvious is the way the sentence plunges the reader into its scene *in medias res*: the oysters have been already swallowed. The shells are "ours," and empty.

I articulate the detail to make something clear. A poem's

comprehension does not require conscious consent. We extrapolate the existence of the riddle, not just its solution, from the clues, in a process mostly beneath the surface of awareness. That this happens in itself surprises: what was the knowledge doing, and where was it doing it, before we knew it was there? Poems share the rhetorical strategies Freud pointed to in dreams: compression, displacement, metaphoric image, pun, and wit. Each relies on the mind knowing more than it knows, more than is outwardly given. And in the case of poetry, relies on the transmission of this surplus of knowledge from one mind into another so tactfully it need not break the surface of awareness to have its effect.

In its second line, "Oysters" turns to metaphor, a device that centers on some unexpected juxtaposition instantaneously and subliminally understood. Good metaphor renews, opens, and extends perception. The surprise of "My tongue was a filling estuary" lies in its joining of human body and body of water, distant in size and conceptual category both; its aptness comes from the recognition of likeness between tongue flooded with oyster brine and riverine inlet filling with ocean.

To read a poem is both to savor its particularities and to make of them a wholeness. On reaching the next unexpectable statement, "My palate hung with starlight," the reader immediately reaches backward in time. We cast the filling estuary into darkness, then see the whiteness shared by both starlight and salt (a brine already present in the mouth, though itself not explicitly named until the following line). But we feel, beyond this, the poem's precipitous increase in space and time, as its images move from shells and plate, tongue and palate, into the planet-scale largenesses of sea, earth, sky, and, finally, myth. We experience further one thing more that is quite counter to ordinary expectations: it's the intimate interior of body and perception that expands to hold estuary and stars. Not only tongue but the self's capacities are altered.

The second stanza exchanges pleasure for the violence eating also is: a rapacity multiplied beyond counting. "Alive and violated" is simple fact for oysters eaten raw, but the grammar governs not only the oysters: it is the Pleiades, the seven sisters pursued by Orion, who lie now as bivalves, opened on beds of ice. In a world whose beings live and die, the savoring of abundance isn't far from the acknowledgment of grief. The stanza's music holds the change as well. Long "i" sounds give way to a short-voweled, single-line abruptness: "Millions of them ripped and shucked and scattered." Parataxis here is speech condensed by pain. By sound as much as meaning, the description foreshadows the anger that later enters the poem.

Next come flowers and limestone, friendship, memory, toasting—a day again close to Edenic. The crockery is unbroken, the thatch unburned. The fourth stanza, though, makes a turn of the kind made formal in sonnets: an addition that both quickens thought and brings a question needing answer. Imperial violence is a subject not broachable by a Northern Irish poet in the 1970s without calling to mind its more proximate history as well. The speaker's welcome coolness under roof thatch now echoes that of the oysters hauled south, under their snow and hay.

The following upsurge of explicit anger brings to consciousness the poem's dialectical range. The consuming of oysters is an act of human and ecological pillage; the communion of friendship in one place cannot erase suffering in another; if there are Pleiades, there is a pursuing Orion who drives them. And yet, consenting to the world we are given is what we do. And more than consent. The day's tang is answered with what Heaney described, in a letter speaking of this poem, as "a certain ferocity or bite called for in our vocation." The promise of the poem's final word leads both toward the action of "verb" and toward what is verbal: a poetry alert to the work of witness, a poet unable to blind himself or be silent before what he sees.

In this example we can see that a good poem's fracture of familiarity and assumption need not be located in a single, large countervalence. The unexpectedness in "Oysters" rests not so much in one extractable concept (though the conceptual and an evaluating moral presence are each sharply present) as in multiple movements of mind which, line by line, are agile leaps in directions impossible to predict, toward a whole not subject to easy summation. Its volatility lies in a balance precise and exacting, momentarily found amid imbalances, both social and personal, that are fundamental, insoluble, and seemingly without end.

The last poem I'd like to inquire of here for its surprises is Robert Frost's brief, adamantine "Nothing Gold Can Stay."

NOTHING GOLD CAN STAY

Nature's first green is gold,
Her hardest hue to hold.
Her early leaf's a flower;
But only so an hour.
Then leaf subsides to leaf.
So Eden sank to grief,
So dawn goes down to day.
Nothing gold can stay.

Robert Frost

Frost's poem is not unlike Cavafy's—a round-form poem in which the end and beginning (in this case the title) appear identical, yet whose readers, going from point A to point A, find it completely changed. As with "Ithaka," the basic counterstatement is set down at the start so clearly and quietly the mind has trouble noticing that it *is* counter: we take in the title at face value, without protest. Yet isn't gold—in myth, in ornament, in religious and cultural reference—the archetype of that which does in fact stay, untarnished, bright against time? The poem's formal structure similarly belies its radical dismantling: four end-stopped and straight-rhymed couplets, mostly iambic trimeter, though the first and last lines each begin with the emphasis of trochee. It is a music of orderly, reassuring recurrence, a poem any child could be put to bed by. So, of course, is "Rock-a-bye, baby"—a lullaby of genuinely

Frostian temperament, with its gleeful conclusion: "Down will come baby, cradle and all."

"Nothing Gold Can Stay" wears the structure of logical syllogism. A poem of premise and conclusion, of data and proof, its first half establishes its *bona fides,* so to speak. Inarguable that new leaves, undeepened by chlorophyll and sun, are not yet green; that the first whorls of an apple tree's foliage are shaped like an opening bud; that these things will soon change. Yet even these opening lines offer the small-scale shock we now recognize as a certain kind of recognition: a making conscious of what was already there to be seen. Frost then begins to quietly alter the contract. Or not so quietly—"Then leaf subsides to leaf" is a dazzling undoing. Its thought is the first to be held to a single, grammatically complete line, and the following rhyme word, "grief," is prefigured by the pattern-breaking pause: diminishment is so strongly felt, no comment can follow. The parataxis, like that in "Oysters," is pain-drawn. A statement that by ordinary logic should be without meaning instead holds perception of loss so large that only spareness can convey it. Yet by any usual assumptions and measure, "subsides" is wrong: the leaf is growing. It is by Frost's measuring as poet, not farmer, that increase is loss.

Each of the following verbs echoes the downward direction of "subsides." That Eden might sink to grief is plausible—the story is after all referred to as "The Fall"—but that dawn *goes down* to day is once again counter to any usual description. The conscious mind doesn't register this as reversal; the heart does. "Inception is loss." The thought is slipped in as only a very sharp knife can be, and one feels the effect only after. Cummings's formulation describes well what this is: a precision creating movement. The poem's change of grammar is also precise, and bifurcating. "*So* Eden sank to grief" moves from leaf-description to a description of suffering in the grammar of logical conclusion (if "so" is read as meaning "therefore") but also in the grammar of example and illustration (if it is read as meaning "likewise"). In the first, the loss of paradise is the poem's focus, in the second, it is no more important than a leaf's change of form. The gesture repeats in the following line. And there is the music, here, too, to be noticed: the repeated, long "e" sounds of "Eden" and "grief" succumb to softly recurring "d"s against the shift of vowels in "dawn" and "down" and then the long-voweled "day."

Nothing gold can stay. The statement's proof lies first with a leaf's small loss of shape and color, then with the fallen world; finally even the day's ordinary increase of physical light is described as a failure, the radiance of all-things-possible becoming merely what happens. By the time the title line returns, the quantity of loss it holds is beyond reckoning. It is not just the outer; it is we ourselves who are dismantled of both our first brightness and the hope of lasting. We, not gold, are what goes. The devastation is beautiful and complete.

.

Beauty is what Frost, and poetry, leaves us. The surprising beauty of truth fully acknowledged, well told and also well tolled—as in, what a bell does; as in, a tally honestly exacted and paid.

While poetry reminds us of the uselessness of the useful, it reminds as well of the usefulness of the useless. It reminds, that is, that existence itself is sufficient. The reasoning of great poetry transcends reason because reason—a faculty rooted in the attainment of goal and its own perpetuation—cannot and does not encompass the whole of life. Through a good poem's eyes and, ironically, by a good poem's craft, we see the world liberated from what we would have it do. Existence does not guarantee us destination, nor trust, nor equity, nor one moment beyond this instant's almost weightless duration. It is a triteness to say that the only thing to be counted upon is that what you count on will not be what comes. Utilitarian truths evaporate: we die. Poems allow us not only to bear the tally and toll of our transience, but to perceive, within their own continually surprising and continually generative abundance, a path through the grief of that insult, into joy.

I began these considerations believing the transcending knowledge of poems is a singularly human liberation; that poetic epiphany, by loosening the psyche from the grip of expectation and purposeful pursuit, is a capacity of knowing entirely unique to our own kind. I still think this is so: if there is a poetry of dolphins, ravens, and elephants, it is not like ours. But something else seems possible as well— that the opposite is also true, that the peculiarly human phenomenon is the grip held on the heart by goal-seeking, end-wedded purpose, and that what good poems restore

us to is something close to what is meant by "animal joy."
They allow us to see the leaf's passage from gold to green
and mourn neither, to taste an oyster for both the history
of rapacity and its salt. Poetry's surprisingly purposeless
purpose, now as in Homeric Greece, is to restore to us the
amplitude and exuberance of the Ithakan journey, even
when knowing that inside a dog it is dark.

Dog (detail)

CHAPTER EIGHT

What Is American in Modern American Poetry: A Brief Primer with Poems

The voice of a culture is made by the tongues and ink of its speakers and writers. Any poetry written in America, then, itself embodies and expands the definition of "American poetry." Within that understanding, Czesław Miłosz, Bertolt Brecht, Denise Levertov, Thom Gunn, Bei Dao, and W. H. Auden each can—and should—be counted at least in part as American poets. Still, certain voices do seem more recognizably American than others, offering some sense of American poetry's distinctive landscape, and of the tectonic plates and local soils by which language, experience, and culture come into the shapes of poems.

A democracy is built on the equality and freedoms of its expression. It seems fitting then to let American poetry speak for itself in its own describing, and to let synecdoche do its work in creating, by sayable parts, the shape and contour of the whole. The few examples that appear in this exploration are necessarily inadequate and arbitrary, holding down the edges of a map they can't convey. Still, their words may perhaps give some sense of American poetry's rivers, mountains, cities, and vernacular breadth.

To begin: Kenneth Koch is a poet whose voice and temperament capture much of what remains central in current American poems. Colloquial, gregarious, observing the self in its relationship to the large with no small allotment of comic proportion, the poem "Movement" comes from fairly late in the poet's life, written after he had traveled to a gathering of poets held on an island some rough-water miles off the southern tip of Chile.

MOVEMENT

Why did I take my life in my hands to see a few fish
And some gigantic cakes of ice
And to meet a few South American writers?
I could have imagined all this without coming here
And slightly increased my chances of staying alive.
I used to think it didn't matter how long I lived
But I didn't know how it did matter how much I saw
And could write about and how many people I met.
I'll have to take my life in my hands again now to go back
From life "down here"
I say "down here" because of the way it is on the map.
I have gone mainly east and south because that's where everything was
*   that I wanted to see.*
Finally, when I was almost sixty I went west, to China.

Where were things I wanted to see but I hadn't known
I could get to with my physical presence
Which is everything, the reason for life.

Kenneth Koch

Good poems require, as we've seen, some reach of being: they move from what's already known and obvious to what is not. All poets travel, then, whether in body or only in mind. Many of the world's poets have traveled for reasons of exile and forced displacement—Ovid, Dante, Po Chu-i, Marina Tsvetaeva, Czesław Miłosz, César Vallejo. Koch, though, moves through the world in the way of the lucky: to see what and who is out there, to test himself against the new, to meet others, to find out who he himself is.

The poem opens in this spirit of chosen curiosity and invitation, with a question whose self-awareness sets the speaker neatly into scale: a figure entirely unheroic, the size of a single, arbitrary, and specific human life. The language here is personal, cut from the fabric of plain conversation, not the more ornate forms ordinarily thought of as "poetic." What this poem discovers, it stumbles into by talking.

This is deliberate. Along with John Ashbery, Frank O'Hara, Barbara Guest, and a few others, Kenneth Koch was a founding member of what's now known as the New York School poets. A century after Walt Whitman first published the book that broke open the ears of American poetry with what he called his "barbaric yawp," the New York School poets, like the Abstract Expressionist painters who were their friends, scraped ideas about art-making down until they could work on unprimed canvas. Their poems sieved the sound of the mind as it mostly lives: unembroidered, unheightened, daily, continually talking away to itself at some subterranean level, often dwelling, as mind does, in the superficial. Yet there's also the unavoidable bumping into reality's cliffs; however casual this poem seems on its surface, Koch cares about, and admits he cares about, what matters.

How does this happen? There's a "Gee whiz" stance in this poem, a background murmur of "Isn't the world interesting? Isn't the mind?" That basic stance marks many of the poets who've emerged from and continue what is basically a New York School style. (A few of the poets not ordinarily associated with this school in whose work its influence can at times be heard are Dean Young, Billy Collins, Marie Howe, Tony Hoagland, Daisy Fried, and Robert Hass.) This is less a matter of subject matter, setting, or circles of friendship than posture. New York School poets wear American hats and pants, shoes good for walking, and love the sound of actual voices speaking; they lean forward a little, curious about the world and how it works. They hold their own stories lightly.

Yet lightness is not the whole of it. The surface innocence of Koch's "Movement" is in the service of something larger, which steals up on its reader with the feet of a baseball player stealing third base: a trick done out in the open, but fast. What Koch's poem tosses out by its end, casually, almost invisibly, is awe—the sheer, implausible shower of luck that existence, in time and place, in world and a living body, is. In this moment of recognition, the poem grows suddenly serious: just past bemusement's border is outright wonder. The poet's seduction is to get you to feel it, while avoiding both sentimentality and self-importance.

Another example of this thinking-out-loud lineage in American poetry is "I Know a Man," by Robert Creeley—a work any living American reader of poems is likely to know. It stays new, and central, by its perfect shifts of pitch and typography, its self-puncturing portrait, and its catching of life and death in a three-dollar hand net.

I KNOW A MAN

As I sd to my
friend, because I am
always talking,—John, I

sd, which was not his
name, the darkness sur-
rounds us, what
can we do against

it, or else, shall we &
why not, buy a goddamn big car,

drive, he sd, for
christ's sake, look
out where yr going.

Robert Creeley

It's worth noticing that this jittery speaker, talking as ceaselessly now to the reader as he did to John-who-is-not-really-John back in the car, arrives at the same bedrock neighborhood Kenneth Koch did. Both poems remind you that you are alive, and might not be. In "Movement," Koch twice explicitly mentions taking his life into his hands—an interesting figure of speech for risking death, since death is what takes us out of our own hands entirely. Robert Creeley's car swerve is a device of hiddenness, happening outside his words' margins—we see it only by the passenger's reaction. Yet the stomach jolts.

Equally noticeable, though, is this: neither poet seems to fret too seriously about dying. Their poems show the same style of being that marks the protagonists of certain iconic American films—think of the untroubled heroes played by John Wayne, Cary Grant, Harrison Ford, Johnny Depp, Clint Eastwood, Bruce Willis, Brad Pitt. (Women actors inhabiting the archetype are fewer, but not nonexistent; Sandra Bullock and Sigourney Weaver at times, perhaps Katharine Hepburn in *The African Queen*.) A signature composure shows up in westerns, war movies, adventure fantasies, romances, films about world-class burglars or spies—insouciance is only one strain of character in American art, but it is pervasive. The steady outpour of saunter and jokes doesn't mean fear is unfelt—coolness only counts if real danger is present. It's worth noticing, too, that both Koch's and Creeley's poems (and the many films of this type) reveal their characteristic temperaments by and in motion. Death's trapdoor is a thing bounded over, escaped by agility, speed, style, kinesis. Abyss is acknowl-edged by looking downward from mid-leap above it.

American culture is founded largely on stories of mov-ing, of "lighting out for the territories," as that equally iconic American figure, Huckleberry Finn, liked to put it. *Moby-Dick* and *Invisible Man*, two other foundational Amer-ican novels, hold equally uprooted and uprooting stories. Both "Movement" and "I Know a Man" carry a home-spun, American take on the worldwide trope of heroic journey. Locomotion—on foot, by wagon, car, boat, plane, metaphoric proxy—is how a person gets from one place to another, from one life to another, and how a poem does. Frank O'Hara famously described the way he thought a poem should be written: "You just go on your nerve. If someone's chasing you down the street with a knife you just run, you don't turn around and shout, 'Give it up, I was a track star for Mineola Prep.'"

I don't mean to imply that the New York School poets' casual, what-comes-to-mind-just-now way of speaking is purely American, or was invented out of thin air by a small group of writers in Manhattan in the 1950s. A similar tone-shift appears in the Beat poets and in certain classical Roman poems, especially those set into the form of letters; and, more quietly, it's audible in Wordsworth's endeavor to bring into poetry the ordinary, shared speech of his age. The intention to catch daily life in daily words (and some larger prey with them) is found also, as we have seen, in the Japa-nese poet Bashō, and translations of haiku and of T'ang and Sung dynasty Chinese poetry changed, in turn, American

poetry's basic flavor. In the opening decade of the twentieth century, poets read translated Asian poetry, available
for the first time to English-speaking readers, then tried to
write along the lines of what they found: a poetry relatively
free of exposition, centered on image, in which much is left
to the reader to complete. One famous example is William
Carlos Williams's "The Red Wheelbarrow":

THE RED WHEELBARROW

so much depends
upon

a red wheel
barrow

glazed with rain
water

beside the white
chickens.

William Carlos Williams

It's difficult to write "in the American grain" (as Williams would go on to attempt quite explicitly to do) and
leave out the self entirely. The first stanza of "The Red
Wheelbarrow," brief as it is, carries into the poem its
author caught thinking: his opinionated, personal presence. A purer example of Imagism's originating practice

is the following, by Ezra Pound, in which the influence of haiku is more directly perceptible:

IN A STATION OF THE METRO

The apparition of these faces in the crowd;
Petals on a wet, black bough.

Ezra Pound

Image here is trusted to carry the poem entirely—but there's also no pretense of American voice at all: Americans generally say "subway," not "metro," and the event this poem distills occurred in Paris. The Imagist movement poets soon moved on, in any case, to other projects. Still, the conscious experiment with writing a poetry of quieter and more transparent speech, in which the subjective self is implied but absent, left a seed style later American poets would return to, and the Imagists' techniques of presentation and juxtaposition were meanwhile thirstily absorbed into other, more complex poems.

❦

To recognize fully the tuning of current American poetry, it's necessary to look back a step further, to Walt Whitman (1819–1892). A newspaper printer living in Brooklyn in the mid-nineteenth century, Whitman set out to invent single-handedly and deliberately a new American poem, one he believed more fitted to the country whose evolution and self-definition were, in the 1850s, still felt as wet clay, a malleable substance. Implausibly, he succeeded—perhaps because his ambition was both a product of and mirror for America's own self-creation. For a direct sense of what Whitman found, here are some of his words, some from poems, others prose. The two often sound indistinguishable out of context, which tells us something about the seamlessness between ordinary language and poetry that Whitman sought.

A morning-glory at my window satisfies me more than the metaphysics of books.

I believe a leaf of grass is no less than the journey-work of the stars.

I find no sweeter fat than sticks to my own bones.

From this hour I ordain myself loosed of limits and imaginary lines . . .

Now I see the secret of the making of the best persons. It is to grow in the open air, and to eat and sleep with the earth.

I too am not a bit tamed, I too am untranslatable,
I sound my barbaric yawp over the roofs of the world.

•

The proof of a poet is that his country absorbs him as affectionately as he has absorbed it.

•

This is what you shall do: Love the earth and sun and the animals, despise riches, give alms to every one that asks, stand up for the stupid and crazy, devote your income and labor to others, hate tyrants, argue not concerning God, have patience and indulgence toward the people, take off your hat to nothing known or unknown or to any man or number of men, go freely with powerful uneducated persons and with the young and with the mothers of families, read these leaves in the open air every season of every year of your life, re-examine all you have been told at school or church or in any book, dismiss whatever insults your own soul, and your very flesh shall be a great poem.

•

Walt Whitman, an American, one of the roughs, a
    kosmos,
Disorderly fleshy and sensual . . . . eating drinking and
    breeding,
No sentimentalist . . . . no stander above men and women
    or apart from them . . . . no more modest than
    immodest.

Unscrew the locks from the doors!
Unscrew the doors themselves from their jambs!

*Whoever degrades another degrades me . . . . and whatever is done or
    said returns at last to me,*
And whatever I do or say I also return.

*Through me the afflatus surging and surging . . . . through me the
    current and index.*

I speak the password primeval . . . . I give the sign of democracy;
*By God! I will accept nothing which all cannot have their
    counterpart of on the same terms.*

Through me many long dumb voices,
Voices of the interminable generations of slaves,
Voices of prostitutes and of deformed persons,
Voices of the diseased and despairing, and of thieves and dwarfs,
Voices of cycles of preparation and accretion,
*And of the threads that connect the stars—and of wombs, and of the
    fatherstuff,*
And of the rights of them the other are down upon,
Of the trivial and flat and foolish and despised,
Of fog in the air and beetles rolling balls of dung.

.

Do I contradict myself? Very well then. . . . I contradict myself;
(I am large. I contain multitudes.)

The investigation of this chapter could simply end here.
These quotes give all the sense anyone needs of what is
quintessentially American in modern American poetry
even now, 150 years later—of its gestures, its values, its

inventiveness, its character, and its source. The briefest answer to the question "What makes American poetry American?" is simply "Walt Whitman."

With Whitman, poetry shook off European-borrowed thoughts, rhythms, images, forms, and conventions, for a poetry rooted in the daily, local ground on which people walked, worked, slept, ate, and loved. With Whitman, American poetry's embrace of inclusion arrives—its optimistic assertion of democracy between all people, things, and beings, its allegiance to the underdog and love of both cities and backwater landscapes, its commitment to openness of border and hybrid vigor. With Whitman, American poetry found its boldness, its compassion, its unembarrassed affirmation of every fate and mood. When William Carlos Williams later wrote a small poem about broken bits of glass in a hospital alley, his attention journeyed in a direction first opened by Whitman, who created a poetry meant to be understood by anyone, with or without education, in praise of every form of existence. When Allen Ginsberg wrote "Howl," the epic Beat poem whose publication in 1956 reawakened American poets to a sense of birthright honesty, scope, and their own boastful grandeur, his line, breadth, and freedom of looking and speaking stemmed in no small part from Whitman.

Nothing in literature is wholly *de novo*. Whitman's own discoveries were shaped dually: by America's founding ideals and the King James Bible. From the Bible Whitman took both his sense of poetry as a vessel for unabashed instruction and his range of diction. The Hebrew, Greek, Sumerian, Germanic, French, Indo-European, and Anglo-

Saxon word stocks that give the seventeenth-century English Bible its astounding breadth are echoed in Whitman's "camarado," "snivel," "kelson," and "kosmos"; in the Bible's translated verses he found, too, his lengthy and ragged free-verse lines. Whitman's democratic and almost limitless allegiances, and the freedom with which he expressed them, have roots in the radical experiment and spirit that underlie the Declaration of Independence and the Constitution. The secular ecstasy and self-celebration, though—these were Whitman's own, mined from the ore of a country he both found himself born into and helped create.

·

American poetry, like Whitman, contains multitudes and not a few contradictions. One is its other founding figure, Whitman's rough contemporary, Emily Dickinson (1830–1886). Reclusive, almost entirely unpublished during her lifetime, Dickinson wrote poems entirely different in voice and aesthetic strategy, but equally distinctive in their newness, poems no less connected to her own experience than Whitman's were to his, and no less influential in setting American poetry onto a path of roughened, unconventional, and idiosyncratic making. Dickinson, too, tested and extended her age's definition of beauty. Dickinson, too, found in herself an unshakable independence of thought and tongue, the sympathetic, unflinching perception of original genius, and a permeability of self so profound that her poems, small as they are in length, turn in as many directions of experience as the plays of

Shakespeare. Dickinson's work includes the outer—birds, snakes, ocean and weather, carpentry tools, an affectionate portrait of a train—but her searchlight focus was interior, the illumination of precise and shifting conditions of mind, emotion, and inner life. As Whitman is expansive, embracer of the large and the list, Dickinson is the anatomist of singular experience, tallied acutely and fearlessly from within.

Dickinson's work does not make a seamless whole—though her ear, line, and orthography are instantly recognizable, one poem's content and attitude can differ wildly from another's. The few, brief examples here offer only a glimpse of this other wellspring of American poetic voice—condensed, elliptical, private, yet in their allegiance to felt experience speaking always of what is also humanly shared. Dickinson's poems, unlike Whitman's, preserve the two traditional sound-driven engines of thought, meter and rhyme, sometimes clearly, sometimes stretched to a faintness so subtle it is more mist of perfume than followable trail.

I dwell in Possibility—
A fairer House than Prose—
More numerous of Windows—
Superior—for Doors—

Of Chambers as the Cedars—
Impregnable of Eye—
And for an Everlasting Roof
The Gambrels of the Sky—

Of Visitors—the fairest—
For Occupation—This—
The spreading wide my narrow Hands
To gather Paradise—

·

Tell all the Truth but tell it slant—
Success in Circuit lies
Too bright for our infirm Delight
The Truth's superb surprise

As Lightning to the Children eased
With explanation kind
The Truth must dazzle gradually
Or every man be blind—

·

To fill a Gap
Insert the Thing that caused it—
Block it up
With Other—and 'twill yawn the more—
You cannot solder an Abyss
With Air.

·

I stepped from Plank to Plank
A slow and cautious way
The Stars about my Head I felt
About my Feet the Sea.

I knew not but the next
Would be my final inch—
This gave me that precarious Gait
Some call Experience.

Unfamiliarity is estranging. Dickinson's poems went almost entirely unpublished in her lifetime, and once in print, many early readers found her work incomprehensible, awkward, minor. Her slant rhymes sounded wrong, if heard at all; her unaccustomed rhythms seemed to limp and stumble. Nor was Whitman's self-published book instantly welcomed. His poetry was declared scandalous, excessive, clangorous to the ear. It did not rhyme, it was unruly and ceaseless, it spoke of every act and part of the body, it celebrated the love of men as well as of women. Yet by his death in 1892, Whitman had become what newspapers called with affection "Our Great Grey Poet," and Dickinson's poems are read now by every schoolchild. Both voices infuse the full range of American poetry, influencing rap, free verse, deconstruction's fragments, rock song lyrics, and the liberations of sound within contemporary villanelles and sonnets.

∼

Poetry's transformational moments are made in words, by "voice"—a term that, when I last looked, seems to be used by writers in a way that does not appear among the Webster's dictionary definitions. Writerly voice might best be defined by analogy—it is the body language of a poem, the way a poem raises an elbow as it reaches for a hat, sets its feet when rising from the seat on a moving subway train, widens its eyes, swings its arms or hips, or doesn't. A stage-hand walks across a stage, to change a set; a dancer crosses the same stage, walking, during a performance—the difference between them is the physical equivalent of "voice" in ordinary speech and "voice" in a poem. The latter is heightened by a performative awareness of its own effect. The body's physical voice is as distinctive as a person's way of running or fingerprint is, and this is true as well of the voice in printed poems. The speaking voice, in the ordinary meaning of that word, has a geographical accent, a family accent; it is shaped by the language it was raised in or has learned. The physical sounding board of the body, it is identifiable as one person's instrument, and no other. The same is true in analogous ways for the voice in a poem and the voice of a poetic tradition. These are sounds, thoughts, worldview made storable fingerprint, visible and lasting because dipped in ink.

What timbres and qualities of pitch and attitude have we found thus far marking the American voice in poems? Openness, curiosity, permeability, hybridity both of being and of diction. Oddness. Speed. Embrace of contradiction, of vastness, of others as not separate or different from self. The self recognized as part of the whole, and at the same time a foregrounding of individual experience and the belief that a single voice matters. "Outsidedness," both of the mind—American poets speak from the edge, not the center, of culture, tradition, and power—and also in a literal leaning toward what is external: Whitman's unfastened door jamb, roads, and rivers; Dickinson's plank under stars. Restlessness, a reliance on movement as solution; a general preference for comfortable grammatical walking shoes over the forms of high fashion. An inhabiting personal presence that's simultaneously central and unimportant. Friendliness, conviviality, affection, transparence—even anger is presented quite often within some sense of and yearning for a larger whole. The surrender of conventions of poetic language for internal murmur, conversation, slantness and "yawp." Engagement, one way or another, with a bedrock real. And most American of all, perhaps, is the undeniable talkiness of American poets, the way they talk to discover who they are.

One other watermark of American art is the search for the new. This is true of art in general—an artist is a person whose hunger refuses yesterday's bread. In American poetics, though, innovation is with noticeable frequency an announced intention—in Whitman, in Pound, in Edna St. Vincent Millay, in the Beats, in the experimental poets of the early 1980s. The attitude may be almost inevitable in a country that was deliberately invented, rooted in a sense of the unknown and new (unknown, that is, to the arriving immigrants, not the violently displaced native peoples). The continent's seemingly limitless landscapes; its strange creatures and plants and geological shapes; its abundance of mineral, winged, furred, and high-branching "resources"—these unfamiliarities reopened both social compacts and possibilities of the spirit.

·

Let us return now to present-moment poetry, with a recent work by W. S. Merwin. The lack of punctuation on the written page (other than that conveyed by the malleable, tactful pauses of layout and white space) is a practice Merwin took up in the 1960s, when he also began to write in free verse. The departure from form is striking, but also silent, and Merwin's clarities are often the clarities of expanded silence, perception made sharper by increase of stillness.

RAIN LIGHT

All day the stars watch from long ago
my mother said I am going now
when you are alone you will be all right
whether or not you know you will know
look at the old house in the dawn rain
all the flowers are forms of water
the sun reminds them through a white cloud
touches the patchwork spread on the hill
the washed colors of the afterlife
that lived there long before you were born
see how they wake without a question
even though the whole world is burning

W. S. Merwin

W. S. Merwin has translated widely, from many languages and eras. A poet who came early to a profound environmental awareness, he has for decades cared for two pieces of land brought back from exhaustion, one in

America, one in France. He has also been for decades a quiet, unannounced practitioner of Zen, and this steady meditation of "just sitting" inside one's own life and its events may be why, remembering the death of his mother, this poet moves nowhere in any external sense, only more deeply into where he already is. In "Rain Light" there is no leaping over, no style beyond what seems plain speech and directness of gaze. Yet the poem's tenderness of observation presents and preserves our human allegiance to the radiance of existence.

American poetry may have hallmark qualities, but among them is this: American poets are not limited or defined by any boundary of style, subject, or provincial accent. At first glance, it is difficult to name just what in this poem is "American," beyond its hybridity—the last line's image brings to mind a central Buddhist teaching. Yet Merwin's lines could not be mistaken as coming from anywhere else. The passport cover stamp here might be found most clearly in the voice: one person speaks on a human scale of what is around him and what matters to him in his life, in a way that's as much a parsing as a setting down. And even in this poem's musical key of inwardness and contemplation, there is American poetry's frequent note of outright, audible speech: the mother's voice, long vanished, is given directly, as well as the poet's own. Where one ends and the other begins is not easily marked—a merging that echoes meaning, as existence itself slips from one generation to the next.

.

Another expansion of American poetry in recent decades has been the inclusion of styles and modes of writing that intentionally elude any purely logical comprehension. There are earlier examples of this—E. E. Cummings comes quickly to mind, and also those American poets who followed the French symbolist poets (who in turn were themselves followers of Edgar Allan Poe)—but the current practice is a more postmodern and less intoxicated probe into the perimeters of meaning and language. John Ashbery is one of the current style's founding practitioners. While other New York School poets—especially Kenneth Koch and Frank O'Hara—traced the movements of daily life in daily words, Ashbery has traced the mind's less coherent, inward ambulations. What follow are three recent examples of this more experimental poetic mode, in which part of the meaning is that meaning itself is placed into some liminal, half-graspable, half-eluding state.

The first two examples are by Jean Valentine, born in 1934 and so a poet of roughly W. S. Merwin's generation. Both Merwin and Valentine were among those who created the "deep image" movement in American poetry alluded to earlier in the discussion of Bashō. This style of poem, which came into prominence during the 1960s and 1970s, joined the Asian image-based aesthetic of uncommented-upon presentation to both the surrealism of Spanish and South American poetry and the imaginative-lyrical freedoms of Rilke, Holderlin, and Goethe. W. S. Merwin took this development one direction, Jean Valentine another.

DO FLIES REMEMBER US

Do flies remember us
We don't them
we say "fly"

say
"woman"
"man"
you   gone
through my hands
me through your hands

our footprints feeling
over us
thirstily

Jean Valentine

ONCE IN THE NIGHTS

Once in the nights
I raced through fast
snow to drink life
from a shoe

what I thought
was wrong with me   with you

was not wrong

> *now*

gates in the dark at thy name hinge

Jean Valentine

The voice here is once again inward and personal, not
public or general; Valentine's poetry, like Merwin's, uses
the rhetoric of an inner speech that feels somehow over-
heard, as if the reader has been granted access to unut-
tered thought. The approach in these poems, despite their
brevity, is fundamentally aggregational, accumulative in
both reticence and disclosure. As in the Robert Creeley
poem seen earlier, Valentine's language is also unabashedly
hybrid in diction: notice the freighted, archaic "thy" of the
second poem's final line.

Jean Valentine's poems carry a sense of seclusion and
an air of the private. They are wonderfully strange, drinking as they do from surrealism's freedoms, and her images
often complicate and baffle. "I raced through fast / snow
to drink life / from a shoe." We intuit our understanding of such a statement. It makes sense, and it does not;
it offers entrance to feeling, but not to full fact. The
"now" late in the poem floats alone on the page, and the
reader stops to ponder whether it belongs with the phrase
above, the phrase below, or if it is a hinge word, belonging equally and separately to both. This last, dual-facing
hypothesis is the reading I myself think intended, but the
possibility for confusion must also be intended: this poem

does not seek the realm of clarities between persons. A kind of pearlescence of both meaning and feeling is at its core.

The signature element that this poetic strategy brings to American writing can be found in the last lines of both poems above: each crafts a beauty and an experience possible only in words, not in the world. In that recognition lies the key to reading this kind of poem. It is poetry's and language's own making we find at work: "now / gates in the dark at thy name hinge." Opening and closure, logic and dream, intimacy and the formality of sacramental speech, all balance on the precipice of intuited knowledge in such a line—a world-making entirely of words' own construction.

Grief in American poetry has many musics. One is fragmentation. In the late 1970s the L-A-N-G-U-A-G-E school and deconstructionist poets practiced for a time a wholesale, almost violent dismantling of meaning— an experiment that might be seen as a kind of ululation accompanying a culture-wide engagement with the "death of the self" not unlike the "death of God" a century before. What was won from the extremes of this nonlinear style is a poetic that is performative, minimalist, discontinuous, and steeply distilled. An example of this voice is a poem by a somewhat younger poet, Catherine Barnett, from her first book, written after the deaths of her young niece and nephew in a plane crash.

(UNTITLED)

C minus A and B equals—
Tree with no branch equals—

What grief looks like:
A knife rusted in the side of a goat.

No, no.
A coin falling in water

And the fish dart for it.

Catherine Barnett

The poem breaks, alters, contradicts itself, can find for itself no summarizing title. What it cannot solve, it enacts, leaving its images to their own balancing act of devastation and gleam. In its speed, sketchiness, and reproduction of the untamed movements of mind, you can say this poem draws from the New York School poets, but in its formal, non-colloquial speech and reliance on presented detail, it draws equally from Dickinson and from the Imagist/ deep image tradition. Yet the sounds and textures here could not have come from either without the passage of American poetry through the nonlinearity of '70s and '80s experimental poetics.

·

A final facet of American poetry that needs bringing forward is its sometimes vexed relationship to public engagement. Whitman wrote directly of the Civil War, of slavery, of building both bridges and nation; Dickinson was, while not entirely silent, quieter on these subjects—though her extreme death awareness must stem at least in part from awareness of the war, not only the more proximate losses of family and friends. Uneasiness about the question of "engaged poetry" has surfaced roughly once a decade for sixty years now, and the debate over whether or not poems should be socially useful or significant elements in larger cultural debate seems, at least for some, perennially troubling.

Other countries have their discussions of this as well, each tuned to its own historical nuance. For many living Chinese poets, for instance, addressing issues of cultural critique and "social realism" was for decades a task imposed by the state, and the idea of writing any overtly political poetry remains anathema. Within that country's almost diametrically opposite historical and cultural perspective, the writing by the Misty Poets about personal emotion and inner life was the transgressive, dissident, and jail-risking act.

For American writers, though, the argument goes something like this: For some who resist what is called "engaged poetry," the feeling is that in an overly pragmatic culture, art should be preserved from an all too pervasive pressure toward utility as the single scale for weighing every conceivable judgment; for others, the poetry of engagement simply seems not good—they feel it is language forced into servitude of a program. As the Irish poet Yeats—himself, we should note, deeply involved with the struggle for Irish independence—once said, "We make out of the quarrel with others, rhetoric, but of the quarrel with ourselves, poetry." On the other side of the question, many feel that the abrasions of history upon, within, and against individual lives have been part of poetry's domain from the start, and that whatever affects a person belongs in poems, and can be joined there to all the rest—the emotional with the intellectual; the personal with the social; the public and the private; the natural world and the humanly made; the coldness of stone and the humanly felt; the knowledge of violent injustice and the longing for lyrical transcendence.

So, for a final instance of current American poetic voice, let us look at a poem that slips the argument's bounds, one that is both politically alert and wholly undogmatic. Yusef Komunyakaa served as a soldier during the Vietnam years and made his first mark as a poet writing of that experience. This poem, though, is more recent. It comes from visiting what is most often called simply "The Wall"—the Vietnam Veterans Memorial's polished angle of black granite, inscribed with the names of that war's American dead.

FACING IT

My black face fades,
hiding inside the black granite.
I said I wouldn't,
dammit: No tears.

I'm stone. I'm flesh.
My clouded reflection eyes me
like a bird of prey, the profile of night
slanted against morning. I turn
this way—the stone lets me go.
I turn that way—I'm inside
the Vietnam Veterans Memorial
again, depending on the light
to make a difference.
I go down the 58,022 names,
half-expecting to find
my own in letters like smoke.
I touch the name Andrew Johnson;
I see the booby trap's white flash.
Names shimmer on a woman's blouse
but when she walks away
the names stay on the wall.
Brushstrokes flash, a red bird's
wings cutting across my stare.
The sky. A plane in the sky.
A white vet's image floats
closer to me, then his pale eyes
look through mine. I'm a window.
He's lost his right arm
inside the stone. In the black mirror
a woman's trying to erase names:
No, she's brushing a boy's hair.

Yusef Komunyakaa

The voice of this poem is midway between private fracture and publicly spoken language. It is no accident that it stops mid-gesture, intimately honoring both the future and uncertainty's tact. Like the monument whose experience it describes, the poem does the work of private and public reknitting not least by acknowledging its own incompleteness—in any experience so enormous and multiple, there will be further unfolding. The Wall holds room for more names than are as yet there. As with each of the poems we've looked at, whatever their verb tense, to read "Facing It" is to enter a present-moment enactment and be changed—we go, with the poet's own transforming awareness, from stone to flesh, from wound to window, from loss to a future able still to be touched with tenderness and moved forward into an imaginably different world.

In Komunyakaa's poem is the individual and the whole,

Vietnam Veterans Memorial Wall

poetry's threshold embrace of inner and outer, many kinds of movement, the contemplation and provisional resolution of estrangement. In it is the American dilemma of race and the American dilemma of war. It holds its subjects lightly, in image, and meets them, turns them over, by power of voice. Many poems might have served to close this survey—poems that equally demonstrate the commingling of qualities sketched out here. But for its complex, tender, direct looking into the questions America faces, this one felt right.

No handful of examples can show the full range of contemporary American poems. There are poets working within highly baroque complexities of grammar and syntax and poets working in modes entirely resistant to comprehension. There are poets who bring contemporary suppleness to traditional forms, poets writing personal narrative, writing diatribes, novels in verse. There are spoken-voice poets, ranging in type from performance and hip-hop to cowboy. There are poets composing postmodern opera libretti and poets writing haiku, Chinese-style quatrains, aphorisms, blues, ballads, ghazals. There are poets who work by erasure, physically blackening out the words of others' writing to cut new meanings into the light.

To speak of what feels "modern" in modern American poetry would require another exploration, equal in length to this one. I will say here only that it is not a matter of poetry's original tasks having suddenly vanished. Contemporary poems keep the art's first ties to oral memory, to serving the needs of cultures and peoples before writing existed. They preserve the abiding strengths of traditional poems—vividness, compression, transformation, witness, negotiation, memorability of sound and expression. But they are also elasticized, compressed, aerosolized, alloyed, plaited, queried by heat and by ice. They include, we might say, more ground. They have been sent into multiple formal exiles, raiding the terrain of dream, of prose, of documentary film, of thrown dice, and called back in an altered tongue. They draw this moment's water from this moment's well. In the realm of technology, modernity arrives with industrial replication. In the arts, modernity arrives through the counterpressure idiosyncracies of individual ingenuity and individual voice; it arrives through both intentional and accidental cross-fertilizations; it arrives as oxygen does, by being what is there to be breathed when words breathe.

What feels to us "American," though, is not quite the same as what feels "modern." The hallmarks of American art are the hallmarks of a culture created by immigration, by mobility of psyche and of body, by the invention required when finding yourself removed from traditional terrain, answers, and ways. Further, American poetry continues to reflect the individualism of its country's founding self-definition: the confidence in one person's, or one small group of persons', capacity to make something genuinely new. It is the legacy of a country founded more in revolution and home-leaving than in continuance. There is, too, the matter of speech patterns, the sense that certain rhythms, sentences, phrases, certain words, have become both portable ground and pocketable seed. And finally, there is the migrant traveler's perennial hunger and search for what can be made known, made home, that leads American poets, more often than not, toward the respite and sustenance of the local and radiant detail—the reflection of a mother stroking the hair of a boy. It is a habit of mind that might well be needed to come into being, when the world is felt as hidden, unknown, and surprising—as needing a first registration in the maps of psyche, language, and heart. The traveler looks for landmarks by which to go forward, and looks also for a place to sit and rest a little, to take in the immensity of what has been, of what may lie ahead.

Maya Lin's original submission for the Vietnam Veterans Memorial Competition

CHAPTER NINE

Poetry, Transformation, and the Column of Tears

Full fathom five thy father lies;
Of his bones are coral made;
Those are pearls that were his eyes;
Nothing of him that doth fade,
But doth suffer a sea-change
Into something rich and strange.
Sea-nymphs hourly ring his knell:
Ding-dong.
Hark! now I hear them—Ding-dong, bell.

William Shakespeare, *The Tempest*

Words transform.

Propaganda is language that steers, hardens, and stupefies. Seduction's words narrow and intensify, arousing one-pointed desire. The language of fact confirms, informs, offers what we hope are reliable bricks for the mind's further assemblings. Directions direct, imperatives order, explanations satisfy, or do not.

Poems can, of course, be turned to each of these ends. But when that happens, if it is all that happens, they become stunted versions of themselves, like plants kept in too confining a pot. As can be seen in even these few lines from *The Tempest,* poetry allowed its full root-run unbinds us, and itself, from all knowable ends.

Poetry's ends are, in truth, peculiar, viewed from the byways of ordinary speech. But it is this oddness that makes poems so needed—true poems, like true love, undo us, and un-island. Contrary, sensual, subversive, they elude our customary allegiance to surface reality, purpose, and will. A good poem is comprehensive and thirsty. It pulls toward what is invisible to an overly directed looking, toward what is protean, volatile, unprotected, and several-handed. Poems rummage the drawers of what does not yet exist but might, in the world, in us. Their inexhaustibility is the inexhaustibility of existence itself, in which each moment plunges from new to new. Like a chemical reagent, water passing through limestone, or a curious toddler, a good poem reveals, entering and leaving altered whatever it meets.

These metamorphic powers are one reason people turn to poetry when they find themselves bewildered—as Dante, lost at midlife in a dark wood—or strongly deflected by some outer event, whether the individual and personal navigations of eros, time, illness, or death; the indiscriminate crises of earthquake, fire, and flood; or the human-made, cultural failures of injustice, exploitation, war. Such events do not ask only practical answers, rational solutions.

When the shape of the outer alters, the inner must shift to meet it, or we will be left in broken incoherence inside our own lives. A good poem turns fresh ground to meet fresh need. Miranda, believing herself fatherless, lives on, and falls in love. Dante goes forward, willingly enters the gates of Hell, by beginning to describe what he sees—in the intimate, vernacular Italian of his home tongue, but also in *terza rima,* in the shaping assistance of poetic form.

Thoughts, like runner beans or climbing roses, are able to travel farther when given both free range and a lattice. Form, in all its conceptual, syntactical, and musical presences, is what changes the mind's stutterings into graspable language, and graspable language into poems. Poems, in turn, transform fate: they make of intransigent outer circumstance something workable, softened.

Poetry's negotiations with fate can unfold in diverse ways. Sometimes poetic alteration is primarily inward, and private; other times, as seen in Yusef Komunyakaa's "Facing It" in the previous chapter, a private poem can also take a more public role. Baudelaire, Whitman, Yeats, Wilfred Owen, Neruda, and Langston Hughes have been at the axis of revolutions both political and social; Edna St. Vincent Millay and Adrienne Rich in the United States, Anna Akhmatova in Russia, and Yosano Akiko in Japan, are among those who altered the arc of women's lives. In either realm, public or private, words are hands, are eyes, and carry their own magnetic and gravitational fields. To say, as Whitman did, "Stout as a horse, affectionate, haughty, electrical, / I and this mystery here we stand. // Clear and sweet is my soul, and clear and sweet is all that is not my soul," is to create an altered relationship between self and other. Such lines are both beautiful and repercussive.

All poems that leave us changed must be, to a greater or lesser degree, what the linguist J. L. Austin named performative speech—language that both summons and constitutes action. "Bless you," we say, when someone sneezes, and she is blessed, or "With these words I do thee wed," and two are wedded. Performatives, like poems, cannot be called objectively true or false, only, in Austin's sweetly avuncular description, called "happy" or "unhappy," "felicitous" or "infelicitous," in their relation to external events. Performatives create, as the name implies, realities of their own making; this, too, as we've seen, is a hallmark power of poetic expression.

Austin, in *How To Do Things With Words,* assigned poetry a special status outside "serious" speech; in one example, he exempts a promise made in a poem or in a joke from the obligation incurred by a promise made to another person in ordinary life. Austin's exception may best apply to the poetry of dramatic monologue. No one believes the speaker of Browning's "My Last Duchess" a self-portrait of Browning. Yet as Emerson said in the essay "The Poet," "Words are also actions." "In a play, the actors cry out / But in the poem the words / themselves cry out," George Oppen wrote. If a performative utterance is defined as the way we alter by spoken words our relationship to self, others, and world, then surely that is what poems do as well.

Czesław Miłosz's "Dedication," written in Warsaw in 1945 and addressed to that city's uprising's dead, is explicitly a performative: it is both poem and the act the poem describes:

DEDICATION

You whom I could not save
Listen to me.
Try to understand this simple speech as I would be ashamed of
    another.
I swear, there is in me no wizardry of words.
I speak to you with silence like a cloud or a tree.

What strengthened me, for you was lethal.
You mixed up farewell to an epoch with the beginning of a new one,
Inspiration of hatred with lyrical beauty;
Blind force with accomplished shape.

Here is a valley of shallow Polish rivers. And an immense bridge
Going into white fog. Here is a broken city;
And the wind throws the screams of gulls on your grave
When I am talking with you.

What is poetry which does not save
Nations or people?
A connivance with official lies,
A song of drunkards whose throats will be cut in a moment,
Readings for sophomore girls.

That I wanted good poetry without knowing it,
That I discovered, late, its salutary aim,
In this and only this I find salvation.

They used to pour millet on graves or poppy seeds
To feed the dead who would come disguised as birds.
I put this book here for you, who once lived
So that you should visit us no more.

Warsaw, 1945

Czesław Miłosz
tr. by Czesław Miłosz

The poem first appeared in a 1945 book whose title I take as also explicitly, directly performative: *Rescue*, in its English translation.

For Miłosz, who had witnessed a ghetto emptied, a city burned, a country occupied, and a culture destroyed, rescue's moral imperative was personal and pressing. Almost seven decades after its writing, "Dedication" continues to charcoal the fingers that hold it. What at first appears to be measured funeral rite, a ceremony liberating souls from suffering by means of offering, reveals itself as closer to desperate measures: the poem is incantation, apology, rebuke, and vow. "You whom I could not save": it is the poet himself, not those addressed, who requires redemption. What this poem offers the dead is less the lain-down book (which the reader must subliminally realize cannot have been printed when the poem was written) than the promise to take up what they no longer can.

"I speak to you with silence like a cloud or a tree," "shallow Polish rivers"—these phrases have long haunted my ears. The words (the English translation here is Miłosz's own) are beautiful on the tongue, with their vowel-play and hush, but they also resist erasure because they carry the moral enlargements of window awareness. As seen earlier in Henry Reed's "Naming of Parts," clouds, trees, and rivers can be trusted precisely because they exist outside our human purposes and violence, outside the intellect's susceptibility to partisan views. Miłosz's summoning of a breathable and continuing physical world allows the reader to breathe for a moment more deeply, inside both an increase of physical largeness and the largeness of suffering.

Window description here also softens bitterness, hardness. A river named by its shallowness is physically specific—and so, more convincingly real—but the adjective awakens tenderness as well. A shallow river is neither forceful nor especially archetypal, it is simply the irreplaceable, valuable, vulnerable presence of transparent water. The images that follow become increasingly foreboding, but the rivered valley proffers a glimpse of an abiding, if fragile, peace. The rivers of Poland and Lithuania remained, throughout Miłosz's life, sustaining and reassuring elements in his poems, the paradisiacal signature and memory of a Lithuanian childhood amid an undamaged nature and undamaged world. It is this recalled, prelapsarian reality the poet decants from the realm of the possible into the actual, by the pitcher of words.

"Dedication" constructs a safe-conduct from almost unbearable pain into the terror and pity of Aristotle's catharsis. Such a poem must surely be seen as performative, as an actual experience, real and consequential as any other. Czesław Miłosz oscillated, as every poet must, when weighing the objective power of poetry and poems, his own especially. Yet he was all his life a believer in prayer, and claimed that Whitman's poems lay behind the First World War—all the young revolutionaries of Europe had avidly read them. These are not the thoughts of a man for whom words are empty of aftermath.

·

While a poem may be performative in its effects, that does not mean its author set out with the conscious intention of enacting some specific outward or inner change. Ceremonial and legal language also transform—but their aim, by definition, is an outcome premade and fixed. The magnetic action of poetry is different: it draws from us what we did not know was there to be drawn. Writers write not to be writers, but to be writing. As we've already seen, predictable epiphany is empty. The known brings nothing new and leaves nothing altered. (If you find yourself perhaps wondering where the surprise can be found in "Dedication," consider that the poem ends in a gesture of not only liberation but something close to exorcism. Dedicatees are not often asked to leave the room.)

The abiding necessity of surprise is one reason that factual recitation alone, though highly effective as an element, rarely leads to the transformation we seek and feel in good poems. The difference between "fact" and "truth," the physicist Niels Bohr once said, is that a fact must be either true or false, while two opposing truths can be equally right, resonant, and informing. For determining facts, we turn to science (or, less happily, at times to courtrooms), but the business of writers is not answers, it is finding right questions. The thought—it is Chekhov's—reminds one of the Hasidic rebbe earlier in this book, and his question-preserving slap. Good poems make clear without making simple.

Poems search for transformation not least by seeking beauty. Beauty in nature and the human-made beauty of poems are not the same. Still, if given a choice between the freedoms of extravagant, bounding, delirious excess and exuberant word-display on one hand, and the dutiful plod of purpose on the other, even nature appears to have voted for the mad-seeming tail of the peacock. The idea of a choice between pleasure and purpose—in art, or in life—is a false one, a Puritan's hat we can choose to wear or leave on the shelf. Aesthetic discovery and evolution are perhaps purposeful in the same purposeless way: each arrives in invention and eros, in the tried-on costumes of rhinocerous horn and sestina, in recombinations mostly accidental and unplanned. Pleasure, not purpose, mates one creature or image with another, and art's seemingly useless pleasures are not idle. They are imagination serving the future in ways beyond will's reach.

What in evolution appears at times to be teleological

can be better explained, scientists say, as change that con-
verges ever more closely on the conditions of the actual.
The same applies to poems. What might at first appear to
be irrational, extravagant peacock's-tail changes in art's
aesthetics and ways of making will be kept for the long
run—as in evolution—only if they answer some pressure,
however hidden, emerging from the actual living out of our
lives. Poems answer questions that matter or are quickly
forgotten. Even Trickster's dismantling devices—chance,
priapic eros, parody, pratfall, destruction, humor—are
instruments of transformation serving survival.

Theater's symbol is two Greek masks, not one. Art gives
delight as well as sorrow, or it could not seduce our attention. It also, as we have seen earlier, gives pause. What stops
us in our tracks recalibrates the psyche. Rilke's "Archaic
Torso of Apollo," a poem that over most of its lines unfolds
as pure contemplation, ends with the famous, startling
imperative: "You must change your life." That the particular statue the poem looks at is fragmentary and damaged,
that much is left to its viewer to fill in with mind, not eye,
is part of its power. The poet, the reader, collaborate with
the marble torso to complete its meaning. Art is never its
own sufficiency. The ground of any artwork's existence is a
human life, psyche, mind, and heart, and the transformations in them it awakens.

Recalibration is equally, if less bluntly, stored in Bertolt Brecht's brief, deceptively simple "Motto," written in 1930s Germany. The poem reads, in full:

In the dark times
Will there also be singing?
Yes, there will be singing
About the dark times.

Bertolt Brecht
tr. by John Willett

It is a truism to recall here Theodor Adorno's assertion, "After the holocaust, there can be no poetry." Brecht's poem answered Adorno in advance; "Dedication," and every good poem written since 1945, refute him after. Yet Adorno's sentence doesn't vanish from cultural awareness, for good reason: the ferocity of its self-judgment is in itself a return of considerative, aesthetic awareness from reeling silence. Rilke's imperative is, in its original context, the psyche's reply to the claims of beauty, but *"Change!"* is equally the psyche's cry before the worst we can know of our human capacity for horror. When heart and mind find themselves utterly undone there are only two paths forward: a new understanding or a self-deadening numbness—and the latter is not a path at all, it is merely continuance. Amid the incomprehensible revelations that emerged from the death camps, Adorno sought some response that did not simplify, evade, or dissemble. In condemning literature, Adorno was doing the work literature does: looking into the unbearable, he responded with words that have long outlasted their original speaking.

Anger alone, though, perpetuates only anger. While the cleansing quarantine of silence may have been for a time what was needed, Adorno's refusal ultimately closes, silences further. Brecht's and Miłosz's poems unclench mind and heart—thus confirming one difference between assertion and poems. In dark times, separation, isolation, and immobility cannot help; strength and will alone cannot help. What restores the capacity for humanness is the realignment that comes from finding ourselves simply, decently, *moved*. For this, we need the connection forged by poetry's singing: words that live on a human voice heard by others, music that underslips the fixities of rational thought. Two plus two will always equal four. A sonnet or string quartet is infinite in its reaching through us.

.

Sing about the dark times, Brecht's "Motto" says. Documentation, in good poetry, is not mere facts, it is fact put into the harness of transformation. What takes stock, then takes public, allows the paralyzed spirit to begin to move. What has been made visible and acknowledged can be held in place, regarded, studied, taken in, moved toward, moved away from. The unfreezing of time and psyche by public recitation, saying aloud to self and to others what has happened—this is the goal of the *Iliad* and of the *gacaca* courts of Rwanda, of the plays of August Wilson and of the truth and reconciliation processes of South Africa and Argentina. It is why the editor of Turkey's tiny Armenian newspaper could say to a small group of visiting American writers, five months after his predecessor's January 2007 assassination a few yards away, "Labels don't matter. The word genocide doesn't matter. 'Genocide' is a red flag to a bull. What matters is that the stories be told, that the young people hear them and tell them. Some Turkish and Armenian young people are now making plays together. That is what matters. We must leave them alone to continue."

The words show how seamlessly documentation shifts into story and art, when the psyche's deep transformation is what is needed. One demonstration can be found in "The War Works Hard," by the Iraqi poet Dunya Mikhail. Speaking almost entirely by means of list and documentation, the poem shows the transmutation of recorded events when they are drawn into poetry's more complex awareness. (The "it" in this excerpt refers back to the title's personified War.)

> *It inspires tyrants*
> *to deliver long speeches,*
> *awards medals to generals*
> *and themes to poets.*
> *It contributes to the industry*
> *of artificial limbs,*
> *provides food for flies,*
> *adds pages to the history books,*
> *achieves equality*
> *between killer and killed,*
> *teaches lovers to write letters,*
> *accustoms young women to waiting,*

fills the newspapers
with articles and pictures,
builds new houses
for the orphans,
invigorates the coffin makers,
gives grave diggers
a pat on the back . . .

And here are the poem's final lines:

The war works with unparalleled diligence!
Yet no one gives it
a word of praise.

Dunya Mikhail
tr. by Elizabeth Winslow

At the surface, the description here may seem detaching, chilling; the voice is not unlike that of a poem seen earlier, Wisława Szymborska's "Some People." Mikhail's overt stance is quietly, subliminally, shocking: we are asked to bring sympathy to this personified War, whose side is rightly unchampioned even by those who wage it, since a victory of any kind would be its end.

The strategies of coldness in this poem are threefold: documentary's rhetoric of objectivity; irony; and synecdoche. A lengthy list almost always functions as a kind of synecdoche (the mind's comprehension of a whole from its parts) because we feel, in such a list, that what is named could potentially continue without end. And so it is here:

Mikhail's list extends beyond itself, to every part of human life and culture. Her lines' objectivity and surface irony are clear. But irony is by definition a false-bottomed drawer, and this poem's effect on writer and reader begins to be felt at another level as well. Over its recitation, stopping at each point of what feels a 360-degree compass, we begin to feel without buffer war's unselective and scathing appetite, the ways in which no one nearby, complicit or innocent, remains untouched. Passing through coldness, we arrive again at heat—and not only because we have been left to feel for ourselves. And then at some further, even more deeply subliminal level, we recognize freedom: a person able to imagine the happy industry of prosthetic and coffin makers is a person not entirely bludgeoned by fate. To write in this way at all, some distance from horror and grief must first be found. This is art's vertiginous leap from captivity to choice, Chekhov's maxim that a writer must "squeeze the last drops of the slave from his blood." Whatever the outward circumstance, a person in the act of writing is chained to neither the condition of master nor the condition of slave.

On one hand, then, poetic transformation occurs by what might be called the paradox of intimate distance. The freedom inherent in art to choose stance, attitude, approach, form, word, is in itself an act of emancipation. When distance increases (as noted earlier, in reading Emily Dickinson's "We grow accustomed to the Dark—"), we often see and feel more, not less, because we are able to take in the whole. And we recognize, too, that the poet crafting the poem is not entirely gripped by the psyche's currents; some part of the self, however subliminally, has stepped back, to know them more fully. This distance allows the reader perspective as well: he or she comes into the poem's experience through the same space the poet-maker has opened.

Still, we are altered only by what can touch us, and so poems offer on the other hand another, quite different kind of transforming intimacy, one that collapses all distance entirely. This intimacy lies in the basic condition of comprehension we bring to the realm of art: in art's transparent rhetoric, whatever enters awareness is experienced as part of, as continuous with, the self. The most recalcitrant object or fact, placed in a poem, is no longer fixed in the outer. It is alloyed with the reader's or writer's experiencing self—inside the body and memory, inside felt expectation, the murmur of music, the lifting or slowing of pulse and breathing. What cannot be immediately—or possibly ever—externally altered can still be brought into dialogue, imagination, and speech.

The experience of art takes place within and under the skin. When we read the word "orange," neuroscientists have found, our taste buds grow larger, more so if we are hungry. A mountain in a poem is known by what has been motionless and stony in us, and by what we have internalized of rock and steepness through legs and eyes. The characters of a story or play are lent our lives' accumulated comprehensions and history, in order to make theirs our own. There is no way to know, in the provinces of art, except by an empathy so profound that the division between self and other dissolves. Inside art, we are subject, not object. Inside poetry, whether its reading or writing, we are, as the Greek word *poïesis* tells us, *makers,* not only of words but also of our own lives. Each of these two modes of intimacy transforms by restoring the psyche to some new-made awareness of aliveness, agency, and the urgency of connection.

∽

One of the roles of poetry, in and after the dark times of crisis, is to remind that a life can keep faith with full feeling, full knowledge, no matter what it has come to see and know. For this, we need to be lured into the condition of being undefended. This is why words that simply open the eyes to war's effects, in an acceptance that does not pick and choose among them, can bring shocked tears to the throat. It is why, in the midst of unbearable circumstance, the window of natural landscape and creatures brings solace. Stepping outside the realm of the human releases the self from its narrowing boundaries.

Beauty unbuckles pain's armoring. Unexpected startlement unfastens the psyche's fortifications, as we have seen. When we set down the narrow, personal story and enter the stories and images of others, the armatures of self-protection dissolve. In the held breath of page, theater, or concerto, we allow what will happen to happen, and this agreement itself is the altering heart of catharsis. To be moved by a work of art is to stand with the cellist of Sarajevo, who during the long siege of that city would bring, each day, instrument and chair to play in a place where snipers routinely killed, reminding himself and others that it was possible to be human, unarmed and vulnerable, permeable to beauty even then, even there. At its best and strangest, it may be that art must live in an openness exposed in every direction.

Any art able to move us holds somewhere within it both the courage and the knowledge of tears. This lubricant knowledge may be deeply hidden, stored in a subterranean cavern, like the Basilica Cistern in Istanbul, built in the sixth century by the emperor Justinian to hold the city's supply of fresh water. Its 336 underground columns were salvaged from earlier Roman temples; one, because of its carved-surface design, is called the Column of Tears. To touch it is supposed to bring good luck. The part of a poem that holds *lacrimae rerum,* "the tears of existence," may be similarly unobtrusive, beneficent, and essential. It may be a single supporting element among hundreds—a catch in the voice, a fracture small as a comma—but it is there, footed in hidden waters, while sustaining the roof-world we travel across and inhabit.

The thought summmons a haiku by Issa:

We wander
the roof of hell,
choosing blossoms.

Kobayashi Issa
tr. by Jane Hirshfield

The column of tears holding up Issa's poem is entirely unsentimental. Lack of self-pity and the paradox of intimate distance allow his small observation to carry an immense weight of grief and compassion. The poem permits moving forward, even in hell-realms, by its Chaplinesque gait of intermingled absurdity, bitterness, and frailty. "We wander the roof of hell"—the initial statement affects strongly on its own, but it is the addition of bending down to pick flowers, that unexpected and soft-handed gesture, that raises a moistening compassion, and transforms the ring-of-iron statement into a music recognizably poem. The scope of the human condition here is balanced midway between the Greek mask that holds tragedy and the mask that holds laughter. To touch Issa's knowledge is also lucky, in the way that any coming into accord with reality is lucky: it frees.

Poems do not need to reverse grief, or to undo or recast history, to do their work of moving and change. There are times when even the thought of solution insults the actual and irreversible truths of a life. Yet acknowledgment of what is, agreement to what is, are companions enough to alter us, inside the unsolvable hour. Here is another poem, this time in an undistanced first-person voice, that looks out at the insoluble with unblinking and yet also unshackling eyes:

MY DREAMS, MY WORKS,
MUST WAIT TILL AFTER HELL

I hold my honey and I store my bread
In little jars and cabinets of my will.
I label clearly, and each latch and lid

I bid, Be firm till I return from hell.
I am very hungry. I am incomplete.
And none can tell when I may dine again.
No man can give me any word but Wait,
The puny light. I keep eyes pointed in;
Hoping that, when the devil days of my hurt
Drag out to their last dregs and I resume
On such legs as are left me, in such heart
As I can manage, remember to go home,
My taste will not have turned insensitive
To honey and bread old purity could love.

Gwendolyn Brooks

Gwendolyn Brooks's confession of impasse, like Issa's haiku, has too direct a gaze to permit self-pity. It carries no answer; nothing outwardly changes in the course of her words—for a black woman writing at the time and place Brooks was writing this poem, change must have looked at times unmanageably far. Yet resolve, here, is its own resolution. The poet's herb of bitter healing is to admit, along with the locked and beaten soul's barrenness, the further pain and vulnerability of hope. Her wish that some part of a feeling self might survive is the lit, cracked outline of a door in a seemingly solid wall; the knowledge that it might not is a throttled howling beneath the poem's surface.

Defenselessness is the gap through which an imaginably different future enters this poem. "Old purity." To call the remembered life by that tender and surrendered name, to recall the shut-away honey and bread it desires—this is the column of tears under lines iced frozen by sorrow but not despair.

The other place a rending appears in these lines is in the two adjacent paratactic statements: "I am very hungry. I am incomplete." The juxtaposition of bodily and spiritual hunger is straightforward and bottomless, and the flatness of their naming is in itself the cut of their sharpness. Duress simplifies speech, as Miłosz says in "Dedication." Pain, at its most pointed, scrapes ornament bare, however much it is also true that form, image, metaphor, are what allow a writer to step from Adorno's silence and begin to speak.

There is a knot here, a meeting of balancing tensions, Wallace Stevens's violence from within that protects us from the violence without. The context of Stevens's statement is not as often remembered: he was trying to describe a close-to-indefinable "nobility" he found almost completely missing from most modern poems, a nobility in which imagination is both fully present and also profoundly faithful to what is real. "Poetry is a revelation made of words by means of words," Stevens wrote in the same essay, while also praising a line from Shakespeare's Sonnet 65: "How with this rage can beauty hold a plea?" Gwendolyn Brooks's poem, it seems to me, in both its beauties and unbeauties, is much about that question. And is noble.

You may have noticed, the poem has also a lattice: it is a Shakespearean sonnet. Sonnet form, like that of the haiku and villanelle, carries the arc of transformation within the DNA of its structure. The pivoting *volta,* or "turn," after the eighth line, demands a deepened and changed comprehension. A sonnet's rhyme scheme is a music tuned to the opening of unlabeled jars, and it is precisely at the start of the closing sestet in Brooks's poem, we may notice, that the word "hope" appears. Yet hers is also, in accord with its subject, a *muted* sonnet. No rhyme in it is perfect. The skewing of "hurt" into "heart" is a truth that comes from the poet's life as well as her craft, and in that, too, is an ancient and long-buried column of tears. Whether or not it is consciously perceived, it is felt.

Definitions of poetry and literature are seemingly infinite and always inadequate, yet we continue to entertain them. One comes to mind: A poem is a cup of words filled past its brim, carrying meanings beyond its own measurable capacity. This sense of uncontainable and mysterious surplus is in each of the poems looked at in this book, and it is also what's meant when we say of an athlete's throw, an animal's leap, a landscape that deepens or stops the breath, that we find it "pure poetry." Poems are made of words that act beyond words' own perimeter because what is infinite in them is not in the poem, but in what it unlocks in us.

Another definition is the one we have been exploring here: A good poem is a through-passage, words that leave poet, reader, and themselves ineradicably changed. Having read a poem that matters, the person who holds the page is different than he or she was before. These two qualities—a distilled surplus and alteration of being—are no small part of what signal *poem-ness*, as opposed to the outer structures that signal *verse.* Even the word "verse," though, upholds the idea that poetry is centered on transformation: the root of that term means a turning. It refers, in its original usage, to the change of an ox's direction when plowing a field; the pattern then came to name the turning lines of writing. Some kinesthetic and visual sense of an animal moving, some scent of opened earth made more fertile, remain among poetry's hallmarks.

Transformation occurs in poems in many ways, and at many levels of scale we haven't begun to explore. Much more might be said of the transformations wrought in poems purely by sound—words that in ordinary speech hold utilitarian meaning alone are made instrument inside poetry's awareness of consonant's rub against consonant, vowel's muted or bright call to vowel, prosody's multiple modes of flood-surge and ebb. There are also the transformations of object into poetic image, by which whatever the eye falls upon or the ear gathers is pressed into larger meaning—as we've seen, a central mode in the haiku of Bashō. There are the sometimes peripheral, sometimes central transformations of metonym, metaphor, and simile, in which the perceptible outer world becomes vessel for the imaginative and subjective. In narrative, story brings change; in dramatic monologue, character unfolds; in ode or metaphysical lyric, a subject is turned and pressed until it releases distilled and expanded fragrance. There are the transformations, too, of hiddenness, in which the unsaid yet present thought becomes the locus of changed comprehension. These diverse aspects of performative transformation are not separate. The effects of poetry are orchestral and fractal, and work by the interconnection of each and all. Each comma, line break, sound-stroke, verb, conjunction, preposition, and noun is part of a poem's transformations of understanding, emotion, and the psyche's reach.

.

What we've been looking at here is not transformation as poetic subject, per se, but the transformation that is held in any poem we find reason to return to, once it's been read a first time. We look to particular works of art, and to art in general, to renew and change our lives. Alteration—a changed state of being, a changed state of feeling and comprehension—is what we have built art's cupboard to store. Something in us wants and apparently requires this, since no human culture exists without its resident arts. One question is, why?

Biologist E. O. Wilson has proposed that human beings possess an innate biophilia, a love of that which, like us, is alive. This affection is experienced as both emotional and aesthetic pleasure, but Wilson places its roots in the most basic pressure of our evolutionary past: life requires life, to live. As deeply innate, I would suggest, is the necessary charge of increased engagement carried by change, by our alertness to and sympathy with whatever alters and moves. A kaleidoscope serves no practical purpose, yet its procession of color and pattern can keep a restless child silent for half an hour, in a state of suspended awe.

It may be that biophilia and the love of what moves are not so very different—one synonym for "alive" is "quick."

What moves—and every change entails some movement from one state of being into another—is felt as part of the community of life. This grant of aliveness is how we fall into the entrancement of shadow puppets on sticks, video games, animated cartoons. Perhaps it is by some generous extension of this affection for the motility of the living that a rocky stream mesmerizes, as does the solitary blinking of an airplane's wing lights crossing the stiller stars of the night sky. The very word "emotion" holds the word "motion."

I would guess, though, that change-awareness itself must be the more fundamental fascination. What moves might be edible or we could in turn be its meal, but inanimate changes are equally matters of life and death. A falling rock, even a path edge collapsed a little since the last time it was traveled, signals danger. A few degrees' rise or fall of temperature is registered as the difference between comfort and distress. In the ancient world, eclipses and comets brought terror. Awareness of alteration is, for any mammal, survival. And the way we know a change matters is by our acute, felt sensitivity to the emotional and aesthetic responses it raises within us: whatever moves in time and space moves also in the realm of our pleasures, aversions, affections. Our eyes find shining things irresistible because they hold, for creatures perennially thirsty, the promise and polish of water.

What engages our human attention most sharply exists—as we ourselves do—in the music and measure of appetite, passion, and time. Whatever repeats in merely mechanical ways soon bores and grows faint to our notice,

as does equally whatever is entirely arbitrary or chaotic. Then there is the Grand Canyon, whose evidence
of change is on a scale of almost unimaginable slowness.
Its walls' recalibration of our human time sense and scale
create an emotional-cognitive vertigo as profound as any
caused by its physical depth. Its rock layers are felt as both
beauty and kin. Subject to the forces of rising and falling,
erosion, erasure, distinction, extinction, the ledges' nar-
rowness and colors' fate are felt on our pulses.

A surprising number of memorable poems concern rocks
and the meanings we take from them, the life we feel in
them—perhaps because the contrast of condition is so
extreme that it must always at some subliminal level bring
surprise. A rock seen in the ordinary way is solid, impas-
sive, inert; yet rocks in poems do strange and unusual
things. Charles Simic's "Stone" charts the difference rather
directly.

STONE

Go inside a stone
That would be my way.
Let somebody else become a dove
Or gnash with a tiger's tooth.
I am happy to be a stone.

From the outside the stone is a riddle:
No one knows how to answer it.
Yet within, it must be cool and quiet

Even though a cow steps on it full weight,
Even though a child throws it in a river;
The stone sinks, slow, unperturbed
To the river bottom
Where the fishes come to knock on it
And listen.

I have seen sparks fly out
When two stones are rubbed,
So perhaps it is not dark inside after all;
Perhaps there is a moon shining
From somewhere, as though behind a hill—
Just enough light to make out
The strange writings, the star-charts
On the inner walls.

Charles Simic

Over its course, the poem moves from one comprehension of stones into the other, assisted by the mind of riddle and some perhaps rather Jungian fishes.

Another poem that alters our view of the lithic is by the Brazilian poet Carlos Drummond de Andrade, which repeats, many times, with the slightest of variations, the simple statement, "In the middle of the road there was a stone." Slipped between is a vow: "Never should I forget this event / in the life of my fatigued retinas. / Never should I forget that in the middle of the road / there was a stone . . . " (*tr. Elizabeth Bishop*). To see a stone fully, then, is to know something worth carrying to the end. The change here is not emplaced, even imaginatively, in the stone at all; it is in the speaker and reader.

For a final example of poetic transformation, here is a stony haiku by Bashō:

Loneliness—
cicadas' crying
darkens the stone

Matsuo Bashō

tr. by Jane Hirshfield and Mariko Aratani

The verb in this poem has been translated many ways—sometimes the cicadas' cries "pierce," sometimes they "soak," sometimes they "drill into" the stone. The literal meaning is closest to what happens when cloth is dyed, when one substance not only enters but alters another. I have chosen here a verb that brings with it that stone-darkening wetness. The exchange of feeling between human emotion, insect, and rock; the interpenetration of sound and substance, surface and interior, momentary and eternal; the released moistness of the cicadas' *lacrimae rerum*—these are the writing on this haiku's inner walls. We might also notice: the one thing the poem shows as shifting—the stone—is the one thing that, in the outer, objective world, would factually not. Yet the infusion of sympathetic response into inanimate rock washes back over both the crying insect and the human who silently listens and looks. That is Bashō's unheroic and almost indiscernible act of rescue. We are less lonely in a world in which one thing touches another.

Poetry's leaps, images, stories, and metaphors are the oxygen possibility breathes. Haiku are effective precisely because their few, spare images offer no explication, opinion, or guidance. Still, Bashō's poem carries an unspoken, unassayable promise: that even in a world consisting wholly of solitude, stone, and cicada, transformation and connection can be found. And these telegraphed, metonymic meanings are, I believe, near the bottom of what can be said about how it is that poems move and change us, before direct saying reaches its limit. They bring hope. They bring community, inscribing into our thirst for connection poetry's particular, compassionate compact, the inseparability of our own lives and the lives of others, of all that exists. They bring tears. And they promise that these are banquet recognitions we may enter and eat of, if we look and feel through even the briefest poem's eyes.

CHAPTER 10

Strange Reaches, Impossibility, and Big Hidden Drawers:
Poetry and Paradox

One of art's most mysterious by-gifts is increase of reach. The quietest poem is not silence, yet its words might add to the portion of silence around them. The most glum poem, in turn, glimmers a little, casting the light by which its own darkness is seen. The poem of luck carries the knowledge of failure; the poem of failure, if it's a good poem, belies its own words, like the man from Crete declaring, "Everything I say is a lie." The word "leaf" in a poem means "leaf," and yet it means something else also—it cannot help but be also green or dry, carry life or dying, connection to or isolation from the larger branch. Things are fully themselves, and as surely are not only that. A book of poems, a painting, is small, a liftable object located outside the self—words are weightless as illegible dust, paint is ground minerals and oil, daubable onto stiff cloth. Yet what is in them enters a person and becomes, as we say, "large as life," and life's waistband suddenly needs letting out. Inclusion of the impossible, the unsayable, and paradox is some part of how the enlargement art brings us is made.

Inventing unreal reaches is a thing humans do. Accounts of the follies and angers of gods, fairy tales, folk tales, Trickster tales, parables, and stories of super-heroic doings are found worldwide. Bears take the name Pooh and begin to talk. Mr. Toad drives a car. We would not universally dream if the imagination's expeditions were not indispensable to any human life. They hold things we hunger for but cannot eat except by feasting in sleep, in daydream, in childhood play, in art. Slaves and prisoners singing of freedom may feel, for that moment, free.

The possibility-hunger in us is both illimitable and illimitably fed. It unfolds most obviously in the plot lines of science fiction films and in the figures of archetypal myths. It lives as well, though, in more ubiquitous and subterranean places, inside devices of expression so subtle and taken for granted that their impossibility underslips any consciousness awareness. Inside these unnoticed fetches of impossible premise and promise, a great deal of poetry's expansion is done.

For a first, seemingly simple example, here is an early poem by Ezra Pound. In it, magnitude of being is released from brevity and spareness as if some implausibly eloquent jack-in-the-box had been loosed from its spring.

AND THE DAYS ARE NOT FULL ENOUGH

And the days are not full enough
And the nights are not full enough
And life slips by like a field mouse
    Not shaking the grass.

Ezra Pound

This seems the plainest of poems: two declarations, one responding image. Yet its four lines feel to me almost bottomless. They raise both agreement and a depth detonation of "*No!*"; they raise bitterness but also some uprush of tenderness, soft as mouse fur or grass, that embraces mouse, grasses, Pound, the reader's own knowledge of unlived hours, the ground note longing for *more* that runs through all beings who hunger. It is very odd. A poem that seems to describe amplitude's failure and despair becomes, in the feeling through of it fully, its own reversal and antidote—a quiet multiplication of the world's largeness.

How does this happen? It must have something to do with the mouse—the reader both watches it go and goes with it—and something to do with the unshaken grass through which it passes. A great quotient of hiddenness lives in this poem, whose image carries, in its homely and small-footed way, the knowledge of all that takes place beneath visible surfaces—unseen, unrevealed, unspoken, yet there. The mouse is also a window image: in its small body, the weight of human concerns can slip away.

But the transformation of feeling must also have something to do with the poem's syntactical constructions. Images matter in the making of meaning, but they come to us precisely, in words whose stitchings-together equally matter. Begin a poem "And," repeat "And," and we will feel the world as addition. Say "not full enough," and in the peculiar, paradoxical semantics of art, which are always inclusive, you have also awakened the mind to its knowledge of fullness. Grass unshaken is shakable, and with it the self of the reader. Whatever is named in a poem comes into awareness, is present even when what's being said is that it's not.

If this seems strange and hard to follow, that's exactly the point. Paradox is the coiled secret, the place in a poem, in a person, whose pressing releases a big hidden drawer inside which much of the real work is done. Hyperbole, the fabulous, the straight-out lies of metaphor and fabricated image—when the impossible enters the mind, the carrying capacity of thought increases. One thing this investigation will attempt to convey is just how frequently, and in how many different hats and coats, bicycles, ferries, and wagons, the impossible does indeed seem to enter poems. It is one reason we sometimes feel ourselves, reading good poems, inside both the realm of the most common human truths and the realms of sequin and smoke, of scarf trick and card trick and mirrors that at once reveal and hide.

Another odd drawer opens for me, in reading Pound's poem—something perhaps not impossible, but certainly far of fetch, given the poem's surface statements and subject. That is: the poem dissolves loneliness, by bringing the confirmation of shared experience. This happens, I think, in reading almost any good poem, though it's only noticed, or needed, when the poem has to do with pain. Pain, at its bluntest, separates and culls, isolates self from others. It lives inside the skin and pulls our available awareness with it. Yet in reading this poem, the ache of an elemental longing is slipped from hand to hand between writer and reader, a coin and token of recognition, and by that transaction, is changed. What was carried alone is suddenly carried by two, by many. The sting here—so deeply interior, so sharply specific a sense of loss it is almost unnamable, except by repeating Pound's words—is recognized, reading this poem, as a thing that is known and felt also by others. The concept of *symbol* goes back to just such a sharing—the word's origin was a coin broken into two jagged halves, which, set back together, make a reunified whole. So it is with suffering, when it meets its own shape in the suffering of others. A fate shared is bigger, but carried by more hands.

·

The most basic devices of poetic speech are themselves, looked at closely, secret compartments, unnoticed places in which paradoxical expansion is stored. Image, metaphor, simile, allusion, music that departs from the metronome's patness, irony, exaggeration, ellipsis, perspective, distortion, compression, disruption, leap, even list, as we've seen—each in some way slips past the narrow blunting of a relationship to the world that is overly literal. These seemingly various Houdini freedoms share one quality in general: each creates and requires a mind doubled, able to take up two thoughts at once. The capacity comes so naturally we mostly don't see it. Yet it *is* impossible: How can a thing say, and mean, both itself and something else?

To begin to see how these doublings unbind and amplify meaning, we might look at what seems the most simple and single of poetry's devices, image. To do this, let us take up for our example one of image's most straightforward poetic presentations: a haiku. This time, another by the eighteenth-century Japanese poet Issa:

> *On a branch*
> *floating downriver,*
> *a cricket singing.*

Kobayashi Issa

tr. Jane Hirshfield

What does the mind do, entering this poem? We might assume it simply takes what it's been given, gathering branch, river, movement, cricket, song, to assemble some one-to-one, mirroring inner perception. And yes, that does happen, and is what would happen in life, were these things directly viewed; any image, in literature or life, is first simply seen, the retina's neural firings "made sense of." But in literature, something else happens as well. Understanding, as we have already seen, is like perception itself is: active, not passive. From the start—it is how our minds work— the listener to a poem is not only registering each word as it arrives but also raising and attempting to answer the omnivorous, subliminal, always present questions of rhetoric: "Who is speaking to whom, in what context, and why?" Or, put more simply: "What do these words want of me?"

This steady, unconscious murmur of question and answer is the way we unfold all language, not only poetry, for its comprehension. In entering a poem, though, we're already aware that what words want from us is something different. A thing becomes art in part by a granted acknowledgment: we are aware that it has been *made,* and made for art's reasons. And so, entering a poem, a person steps at once into at least two rhetorical frames. There's the frame of the particular poem's particular speaking, and there's also the deeper frame of poetry itself, the shifted background knowledge that these words are a poem, and that in them a poem's maker is speaking to a poem's listener, within poetry's forms and intentions. From the first syllable, then, we look for those forms and intentions: for words that sing as well as speak, for words that hear as well as speak, for thought and feeling unfrightened of depth and complication, for intensification, for implication, for playfulness, for all the surplus marks that increased attention leaves on language, which we call meaning, call pleasure, call beauty, call tenderness, call, sometimes, terror. Within this kind of listening, Issa's cricket is both cricket and *image*.

Rhetoric offers us a changed compact, when we enter the realm of art: it offers freedom. Practicality takes down its guard stations at art's borders, skepticism is traded for permeability and entrancement. Frank O'Hara wrote in *Lunch Poems* of the poems of Pierre Reverdy, "I love Reverdy for saying yes, though I don't believe it." What in science or logic is impossible, in poetry is daily as bread. Like Lewis Carroll's White Queen, a good poem thinks six impossible things before breakfast.

In drama, this condition of mind is named "the willing suspension of disbelief." Less often recognized is that all art forms require this. Perhaps because drama looks more like our ordinary lives, with life-size, visibly breathing people acting and speaking in a room we share with them, it has somehow seemed more pressing to recognize explicitly that what occurs on the stage is a fiction—a person must learn that the swords are not real and that the audience need not rush to put out the fire. (This initial, powerful entrance into a fictional compact is why "breaking the fourth wall" in drama never loses its power: a rhetorical rug is being pulled out from underfoot.) Still, what we are trying to investigate here is something more subtle still. It is the way certain kinds of language involve wholesale, unconscious surrender of our customary, useful skepticism. In art, we seek something else: possibility opened to a vastly increased range of swing.

A few philosophers, linguists, and critics have begun to investigate the metacognitive condition of literature, using terms such as "possible worlds theory," "fictional worlds," and "fictionality." (Of their books, the first to read might be Thomas G. Pavel's *Fictional Worlds*.) The field is only tangentially related to the more familiar "possible worlds" of quantum physics, and the term includes but means something quite different from the "possible worlds" of science fiction. These possible-world analyses of literature speak more in the language of ontological status and "altered awareness" (in a specialized sense) than of rhetoric. Yet the dynamics of malleability they are engaged with are profoundly a part of how rhetoric works.

Literacy (the capacity to turn thought into objective symbols) exists to foil time. Writing sets ideas and information into a form objectively stable, safely outside individual, humanly fragile, self-serving memory. *Literature* is different. It exists to find and hold what cannot be found or retained by other means. And this is yet another way that poetry enlarges: its mapmaking takes place past the edge of the physical page.

The location explains why poems seem so often to look both at what is most central and what seems most off to the side, emotionally, conceptually, economically, politically, ethically, spiritually. In certain archaic cultures, anthropologists report, what matters is less the border between "real" and "fiction" than the one between the insignificant and the memorable. In poetry, where the insignificant so often becomes the memorable, this distinction is not archaic at all—it's one of the few that count.

This thought leads us finally back to Issa's small branch and smaller cricket, a haiku found memorable for more than two hundred years.

On a branch
floating downriver,
a cricket singing.

Entering Issa's image within art's doubled, inquiring awareness, we still find cricket is cricket, branch is branch, floating is floating, river is river. The scene is a long-vanished, insignificant glimpse—and yet its currents hold something immediate and charged. This contrast of importance-scale is in itself a part of many haikus' meaning: attention's recalibration lies at the center of this brief poetic form. We might think also, considering Issa's poem, of William Carlos Williams's "no ideas but in things" (an aesthetic position Williams came to after reading early-twentieth-century translations of Chinese and Japanese poems). The paradox of this much-quoted phrase isn't meant to direct toward a poetry (or toward a self) without ideas or feelings. It does suggest that object and image can be trusted to carry the work of heart and of mind. A kite needs its held string to fly, and ideas need the primary world. When we give ourselves over to seeing a thing completely, ideas and feelings will be there to be found; when we find ourselves captured by ideas and feelings, they can often be spoken to others most clearly by the universally available language of object and image. This is the basis of image's work in the psyche, and is also the core of its sometimes perplexing suppleness: for different readers, in different moods, which feelings are found in this haiku will vary.

The archetypal understanding of rivers, in dreams and in art, is time and journey, the course of a life. Mostly we understand a cricket as a negligible yet noticeable part of existence, some small, unimportant, loud-voiced, short-lived thing. A branch on a tree blossoms or fruits, leafs out, supports, houses, extends . . . but what is a branch in a river? This is harder to say, but surely it has something to do with something fundamentally out of place: neither branch nor cricket in this haiku belongs where it is. Singing: in nature, most often a signal of safety. Courtship and self-announcement take place in places and times free of peril. And in poems, song usually signals joy, ease, the pleasure of praise.And so, in this poem something short-lived and unimportant is found in the midst of a highly precarious condition of existence—and it is singing. To sing as you're being swept down a river can seem gallant, or foolish. The thought of the orchestra members continuing to play as the *Titanic* foundered seems not unrelated, and raises similarly varied responses. Or, for yet another possible tangent of response, there is the conclusion of Camus's famous essay: "One must imagine Sisyphus happy."

Issa's haiku can be taken as an image of the transience and susceptibility of any life at any moment. It can be taken as a portrait of that same, fleeting moment expressing its fullness completely, regardless of danger, fragility, and transience. In some moods of reading, this haiku is bitter, in other moods, joyous.

None of these interpretations is right or wrong, all are possible, all are self-portraits for whoever looks in the moment of looking. That protean multiplicity of possibility is another quality of poetry's complex relationship to meaning and its freedoms as well. Multiplicity of line, of direction, of view, is a drawing's cross-hatched rounding. Experience doesn't arrive inscribed with interpretation. The plenitude of response to these three lines is revealing, and a paradox in itself: how can it be that a poem so seemingly particular, small, and specific is so broadly open to multiple responses?

·

To see if this hypothesis of amplitude and impossibility's connection will hold, let us turn to a poem different in almost every dimension from the two we've looked at so far: "The Map," the first poem in Elizabeth Bishop's first book.

THE MAP

Land lies in water; it is shadowed green.
Shadows, or are they shallows, at its edges
showing the line of long sea-weeded ledges
where weeds hang to the simple blue from green.
Or does the land lean down to lift the sea from under,
drawing it unperturbed around itself?
Along the fine tan sandy shelf
is the land tugging at the sea from under?

The shadow of Newfoundland lies flat and still.
Labrador's yellow, where the moony Eskimo
has oiled it. We can stroke these lovely bays,
under a glass as if they were expected to blossom,
or as if to provide a clean cage for invisible fish.
The names of seashore towns run out to sea,
the names of cities cross the neighboring mountains
—the printer here experiencing the same excitement

as when emotion too far exceeds its cause.
These peninsulas take the water between thumb and finger
like women feeling for the smoothness of yard-goods.

Mapped waters are more quiet than the land is,
lending the land their waves' own conformation:
and Norway's hare runs south in agitation,
profiles investigate the sea, where land is.
Are they assigned, or can the countries pick their colors?
—What suits the character or the native waters best.
Topography displays no favorites; North's as near as West.
More delicate than the historians' are the map-makers' colors.

Elizabeth Bishop

The alchemies of expansion here are entirely different
from those seen in Pound's and Issa's poems. "The Map"
is of course longer and more complex. More central a difference, though, is that the conceptual terrain is not that
of pure image. The poem is filled with striking images,
but their use is—as in the cognitive strategy of maps
themselves—symbolic and metonymic. The poem ponders
abstraction, and abstraction's place between mind and the
real, but it does not do this abstractly. Its lines are a hub of
the actual. They are as saturated with life as a painting by
Breughel—or more accurately, a painting by Bosch, since
looked at closely, Bishop's realisms kilter.

Poetry stands in an odd relationship to reality, to mirror
and maplike reduction, to other kinds of complexity and
simplification. Logic, mathematics, and applied physics

simplify for practical purposes. Their models, elegant and at times beautiful to those in the field, are independent of mood, and have no weather: they strip detail, specificity, subtlety, shadings of feeling. Art simplifies and selects, but does not reduce; it focuses concentration in order to see more fully, at greater depth. We feel this in poems as keenly as we do in certain paintings—when looking, for instance, at four small apricots or a bundle of tied white asparagus, seen through the eye and hand of Adriaen Coorte.

Still Life with Asparagus

Take Bishop's first, seemingly obvious statement: "Land lies in water; it is shadowed green." This might be literal, an accurate description of a looked-at map, or equally, if we were to ignore the poem's title, a description of the landscape itself. It feels almost a painting—but it is a poem, and so tuned to pleasures both within and beyond those of immediate seeing. The mind accustomed to reading images for their Jungian parsing might, for instance, think of consciousness surrounded and altered by the deeper unconscious. The ear alert to poetry's music might hear the alliterative "l"s of "land lies," might follow the "a" moving through "land," "water," and "shadow" for the transformation of understanding that unfolding offers, might take in the long, slowing emphasis of the arrival of the "e" in "green." Awareness attuned to such transformations might pause, take breath, wonder: What next? And what's next does not disappoint: "Shadows, or are they shallows . . . ?" Bishop inquires. The question, simultaneously thought-born and sound-born, lives in elements both objective and subjective. Is this a question of psyche or of literal perception, we might wonder. And then: Is there a difference?

Almost every line in "The Map" carries a visibly doubled awareness. (Or more correctly, a tripled awareness, as we bring, in addition, the basic awareness of "poem-ness" that invites further levels to emerge at all.) This poem ponders actual maps and ponders maps as a figure for art's navigations. It looks at topography's recording and it looks at subjective experience, at the act of recording. Bishop's customary strategy of asking questions, of double-checking thought and perception, can't help but summon the reader to sharpened alertness. To read a poem by Bishop is to enter a state almost Kabbalistic. We become more subtle, precise, alive, when words act as both depository and request for attention. Put flatly: good poems make us smarter.

"The Map" is too long, too strange and meticulous, to explore here completely, yet irresistible not to rummage in further. There's the message-in-bottle, for instance, to be found in its formal structure. The first and third stanzas make a *sui generis* pattern, eight lines chalked out sometimes by the more usual kinds of rhyme, sometimes by a word's exact repetition. Such repetition (welcomed in Urdu) is generally frowned on in English sound-work. Bishop's use of it lets readers know at once: we are in the hands of a writer both ruly and unruly, deliberate but not deferential. This first poem in a first book is by a writer who will follow and abandon custom as she pleases, working by her own likings for what she makes.

Between the two orderly border stanzas, the central one ranges more loosely in structure. The poem's structure, then, echoes that of maps in general, whose strongest information concerns setting boundary and edge. The second, middle stanza here—like the places in maps between lines—is humanly inhabited. Disorderly and cluttered, it holds towns and countries with overlong names, the man-made substances of glass, cage, oil, and yard goods, women gone shopping. It is also the only place in the poem where a first-person pronoun and view can be found. This is explicit in the "we" and perhaps also inhabits the printer, an occupation that can be seen as placeholder for the writer. I can't help but wonder if some protective affection hasn't placed them all, contained and surrounded yet free in themselves, to wander between form's stricter lines. When established customs are broken, it's worth asking why, in a poet for whom we can trust no decision is careless.

Does all this seem impossibly subtle? It is, and is not.

We might next notice Bishop's quietly extreme personifications—the primary reason I chose this poem to look at here. Each demonstrates just how easily and casually the impossible strolls through a poem, almost unnoticed—land gathers sea around it as a person might pull close a shawl; peninsulas finger water as if women testing the quality of cloth; an inked outline runs off as a rabbit. These image-metaphors, more verb than noun, remind that the root meaning of "vivid" is "alive." We read them, and register only the pleasure of something new, not seen before. Yet none, looked at closely, is short of completely fantastic, in the original sense of that word. They are working impossibilities all.

Finally, consider the poem's last line: "More delicate than the historians' are the map-makers' colors." Even this quiet statement holds doubled meaning. What is delicate is not only subtle, it is also fragile, susceptible to circumstance, easily changed. The line reminds that we're in the realm of the made and distilled (historians do not work with "color"), of intelligence and judgment, and also of choices that haven't been hard set as yet, and perhaps can't be. Provisionality, self-questioning, the reframing awareness of awareness, watermark Bishop's poetry from start to finish. Her lines register a handmade authority, one drawn with almost-erasable artist's charcoal, not ink. This stance of continuously revised speculation is Bishop's most characteristic technique for moving perimeter outward. Asking and answering questions, she can say almost anything—"moony Eskimo," "clean cage for invisible fish."

The volume and tone are so measured, we hardly notice the full flamboyance, and never protest it. The combination recalls James Merrill's description of Bishop herself: an "instinctive, modest, life-long impersonation of an *ordinary woman*."

Among the many paradoxical ways good poems enlarge the world is another dimension yet: their own sheer proliferance. No matter how many poems exist, there is, it seems, always room for another—another mode, form, diction, subject, view. Poems make new reaches of language and feeling the way evolution makes new hooves, air bladders, ankles, tails, and scents. If they last, as we have seen, it will be for the same reason: because they're both useful and needed. The table of art is infinitely expandable—any good poem can set itself a new place. In this way, poems are like life itself: an ever-increasing inhabitance of the possible, a realm in which something else is still able to happen.

Art is the realm in which, perhaps, *anything* can. As the Brazilian poet Manoel de Barros describes this fecundity in a section of his "Self-Portrait": "I produced unobjects . . . / Let me cite the most worn: a milky scissor, / a dawn opener, a buckle / for fastening silences, a tack that crackles, / a velvet screw, etc. I have a confession: / ninety percent of what I write / is invention; only ten percent is a lie" (*tr. Idra Novey*). This allegiance to endless possibility is found in good novels, plays, paintings, musical compositions, and poems. Art makes open cases, not closed ones, and, as we've seen, keeps speaking beyond the point where speech that's hearable ends. Art's goal is not the end-stop of a mathematical formula solved, a chemical reaction exhausted. It is to leave us holding a box that can't ever be entirely sealed or put away.

Often, this paradox of ending-that-does-not-end is out in the open. Elizabeth Bishop's "The Fish" famously closes "And I let the fish go." Two lives continue past that statement, undescribed. Another example of unsealed closure—and example, too, of paradox, hyperbole, personification, and impossible assertion piled on impossible assertion in undisguised glee—is W. H. Auden's "As I Walked Out One Evening."

AS I WALKED OUT ONE EVENING

As I walked out one evening,
  Walking down Bristol Street,
The crowds upon the pavement
  Were fields of harvest wheat.

And down by the brimming river
  I heard a lover sing
Under an arch of the railway:
  "Love has no ending.

"I'll love you, dear, I'll love you
  Till China and Africa meet,
And the river jumps over the mountain
  And the salmon sing in the street,

"I'll love you till the ocean
    Is folded and hung up to dry
And the seven stars go squawking
    Like geese about the sky.

"The years shall run like rabbits,
    For in my arms I hold
The Flower of the Ages,
    And the first love of the world."

But all the clocks in the city
    Began to whirr and chime:
"O let not Time deceive you,
    You cannot conquer Time.

"In the burrows of the Nightmare
    Where Justice naked is,
Time watches from the shadow
    And coughs when you would kiss.

"In headaches and in worry
    Vaguely life leaks away,
And Time will have his fancy
    To-morrow or to-day.

"Into many a green valley
    Drifts the appalling snow;
Time breaks the threaded dances
    And the diver's brilliant bow.

"O plunge your hands in water,
    Plunge them in up to the wrist;
Stare, stare in the basin
    And wonder what you've missed.

"The glacier knocks in the cupboard,
    The desert sighs in the bed,
And the crack in the tea-cup opens
    A lane to the land of the dead.

"Where the beggars raffle the banknotes
    And the Giant is enchanting to Jack,
And the Lily-white Boy is a Roarer,
    And Jill goes down on her back.

"O look, look in the mirror,
    O look in your distress:
Life remains a blessing
    Although you cannot bless.

"O stand, stand at the window
    As the tears scald and start;
You shall love your crooked neighbour
    With your crooked heart.'

It was late, late in the evening,
    The lovers they were gone;
The clocks had ceased their chiming,
    And the deep river ran on.

                                        W. H. Auden

This poem's ample impossibilities need no naming to be seen, or for their effects of collision-enlargement to be felt. The count of glaciers in its cupboards is, conservatively, twenty-seven. Auden summons as well another form of paradox, one we might label aesthetic rather than conceptual, in his cross-use of tone: adult complication is held by fairy-tale diction and nursery-rhyme lull. The poem's desolation is all the more chilling for that contradiction of substance and surface. But who would analyze or explicate Auden's lines, given the chance simply to say them again? I will only recall why the poem appears just here: to notice how its end does not close shut entirely. That cold, deep, on-running river is both knife held to the throat of human love and, however bleakly felt, a sliver of narrowest reprieve from that knife as well.

·

Ezra Pound's four-line poem chafes at the undone, the unlived through; Auden's is equally bleak on the subject of time; Issa's and Bishop's, in different ways, step outside time's pressure completely. A four-line poem by the Polish poet Julia Hartwig, now in her nineties, finds in unfinishedness—perhaps in unfinishableness—wealth. For Hartwig, the uncompleted is welcome in the way an open door is: it is a gap, one that anything might walk through. The title of the collection that includes this poem states its theme even more succinctly: *In Praise of the Unfinished.*

FEELING THE WAY

The most beautiful is what is still unfinished
a sky filled with stars uncharted by astronomers
a sketch by Leonardo a song broken off by emotion
A pencil a brush suspended in the air

Julie Hartwig
tr. by John and Bogdana Carpenter

A single abstract declaration is followed by four quick image-examples, each doing its own compressed work. Uncharted stars, the pencil and brush suspended: these are metonyms for the possibility the incomplete points toward. The poem's absence of punctuation is an open selvage as well, in place of what would ordinarily be finished seam. Hartwig's summoned Leonardo sketch is a concept that travels in multiple directions and dimensions. I myself think of it first as some abandoned idea, which, in the case of Leonardo, a genius so prolific that most of his realizations would be left to notebook and future, surely acts as a trope for richness. But it also suggests suggestion itself— the quick lines by which da Vinci conveyed a rearing war horse, the idea of a helicopter, a mother's love for her child.

That a few lines drawn on paper can evoke actualities of world and psyche is another of art-making's fundamental paradox-riddles: How is it that, in art, less so often is more? Something related underlies Hartwig's "song broken off by emotion"—silence washes back into the unheard voice and charges it further. What overpowers and fractures will carry more strength of feeling than anything artfully completed—another paradox-truth to ponder. The overflow quickens Hartwig's poem to its own near absence. Its idea touches down like some small, intelligent, nervous bird, and departs. The poem's largest paradox, though, is far out in the open: Hartwig's embrace of the broken-off as trope for possibility rather than death.

Many writers have described both the depth and the necessity of language's unfilled places. "What is important," the Swiss novelist Max Frisch wrote, "is what cannot be said, the white space between the words." The Czech poet Miroslav Holub said in a *Paris Review* interview, "In a broader sense, all poetry aims for the silence between and after the words . . . Poetry should use a minimum of words for a maximum of conceived silence." And then there is Emily Dickinson: "I dwell in Possibility— / A fairer House than Prose— / More numerous of Windows— / Superior—for Doors—"

In this understanding, incompletion and the unsaid are not failure, they are a way to house what is otherwise too large for housing. Good poems have an uncanny ability to have it both ways, and Hartwig's words mirror what they describe. They amount to barely a sketch, yet they make visible, touchable, what cannot be held by closed fingers: the vastness around them.

·

To finish this tour of paradox and expansion, let us look at two poets in a relatively unusual condition for poets, at least in their poems: they are happy. Few good poems are capable of shepherding happiness onto the page, just as relatively few (are there any?) are capable of holding entirely untroubled love. Grief is simpler. There, word-beauty and world-lure provide the counterweight ballast: if we're still breathing and speaking, that is evidence of wanting to live. The writing of happiness requires its own counter-pull gesture—some part of the poem must doubt its own saying's lasting.

Here, first, then, is an early poem by Frank O'Hara.

TODAY

Oh! kangaroos, sequins, chocolate sodas!
You really are beautiful! Pearls,
harmonicas, jujubes, aspirins! all
the stuff they've always talked about
still makes a poem a surprise!
These things are with us every day
even on beachheads and biers. They
do have meaning. They're strong as rocks.

Frank O'Hara

And here is a late poem, unpublished during his life, by Raymond Carver:

SODA CRACKERS

You soda crackers! I remember
when I arrived here in the rain,

whipped out and alone.
How we shared the aloneness
and quiet of this house.
And the doubt that held me
from fingers to toes
as I took you out
of your cellophane wrapping
and ate you, meditatively,
at the kitchen table
that first night with cheese,
and mushroom soup. Now,
a month later to the day,
an important part of us
is still here. I'm fine.
And you—I'm proud of you, too.
You're even getting remarked
on in print! Every soda cracker
should be so lucky.
We've done all right for
ourselves. Listen to me.
I never thought
I could go on like this
about soda crackers.
But I tell you
the clear sunshiny
days are here, at last.

Raymond Carver

Each of these poems, in quite different ways, holds some undertow shiver and backward lean; in each, happiness looks back a little over its shoulder. In Frank O'Hara's poem, the first hint appears in the title. If this is "Today," what of the other days, what of tomorrow once today passes? The more defined a period of time, the more we feel it is vulnerable, subject to transience. The larger evidence of undertow, though, and what erases any doubt that undertow is present, is the poem's reference to biers and beachheads. O'Hara served in the Second World War, whose graves and sites of carnage those words remember. The experience comes back again, more subtly, in the poem's last line. What can it mean to say so improbably of kangaroos, jujubes, aspirin, and sequins "They are strong as rocks"? Rocks are, for the sonar operator of a destroyer (as O'Hara was), an unforgiving danger. For anyone, they are cold, immobile, inanimate, and the obdurate opposite of sequins and aspirin. The statement places the trinkets and the minor next to death, measures both, praises both, and calls them equal—which is indeed the most generous possible grant of any day's meaning.

Raymond Carver's celebration of soda crackers also holds implausibility out in the open. Soda crackers are plain, the offering of a minimal cupboard, and odd to find celebrated in an ode. However much we've grown used to unexpected praisings after Neruda's outpouring of odes to socks, ticking watches, and dead fish in the market, familiarity can't block the initial surprise: the coupling of extraordinary and meager will always be found peculiar. A soda cracker is even stranger when chosen as something to speak to directly. I asked Tess Gallagher, Raymond Carver's widow, about this poem, wondering if the crackers might have had some special meaning at the end of his life. She answered no, then added, "I think soda crackers are just a staple in working-class houses, so you are likely to find them in a scantly supplied place and be assured you won't go hungry. They are 'saving' food. My generation grew up with them in our chili and soup."

By the time I received Gallagher's answer, I'd already realized the poem's meaning would be unchanged, whatever she said. "An important part of us is still here. I'm fine"—abyss lies under that statement either way. The announcement "I'm fine," when made in a poem, declares "I might not be," just as the declaration "I tell you, the clear sunshiny days are here at last," informs us that Carver knows well that lasting is not the way of days. ("Sunshiny"—what a sublimely self-skeptical adjective, made simply by adding a "y.") Lies need assertion; truths take care of themselves.

Each of these poems gives full space to both sides of amplitude's making. Both hold immunization against self-deception. Raymond Carver really is happy, even knowing full well it won't last. Frank O'Hara's allegiance is to both rock and joy. A person able to put two knowledges into one funny, handmade, awkward word is a person who might take on—vulnerably, expansively, happily—that most impossible of human questions: how we go on at all, knowing each beloved unfinishedness will finish, without us. Impossible to ponder. Done every day. Sometimes with crackers.

ACKNOWLEDGMENTS

I am grateful to the editors of the journals in which some parts of this book have previously appeared: *American Poetry Review, Associated Writing Programs Chronicle, Orion,* and *World Literature Today.* The chapter "Seeing Through Words: An Introduction to Bashō, Haiku, and the Suppleness of Image" first appeared as an Amazon Kindle Single e-book, *The Heart of Haiku.* Three chapters here, first delivered as the Bloodaxe Lectures at Newcastle University, appeared in much earlier form in *Hiddenness, Uncertainty, Surprise: Three Generative Energies of Poetry.*

Many of the thoughts in this book began with invitations over the past twenty years to talk about poetry with others. My thanks go to the Bread Loaf Writers Conference; the Napa Valley Writers Conference; the Key West Literary Seminars; Bennington College's MFA Writing Seminars; the Crossing Borders symposium hosted by Nanjing University of Posts and Telecommunications and the Nanjing campus of the New York Institute of Technology; Fudan University (Shanghai); Dokkyo University (Tokyo); and the request to speak about Bashō for the Poetry in the Branches program of roving lectures in public libraries, cosponsored by Poets House and the Poetry Society of America.

My gratitude also to Deborah Garrison, Annie Eggers, and all those at Knopf, and beyond, who have contributed to the book you now hold in your hands.

Grateful acknowledgment is made to the following for permission to reprint photographs:

p. 37 (top): Photo by Donald Glaser, used by permission of the Lawrence Berkeley National Laboratory

p. 37 (bottom): Photo by Donald Glaser, used by permission of Lynn Glaser

p. 47: © Pierre Terre; photo used under Creative Commons License 2.0. Source: http://www.geograph.org.uk/photo/949593

p. 81: © 2011 Jane Hirshfield

p. 95: Kyoto file photo from Wikimedia; photo used under Creative Commons License 2.5. Source: http://en.wikipedia.org/wiki/File:Kyoto-Ryoan-Ji_MG_4512.jpg

p. 134: Photo used under Creative Commons License 2.0. Source: http://ja.wikipedia.org/wiki/%E3%82%B5%E3%82%A4%E3%82%B3%E3%83%AD

p. 191: Photo used under Creative Commons License, 3.0. Source: http://en.wikipedia.org/wiki/File:Times_Square_112808%282%29.jpg

p. 238: Photo by Derek Key, photo used under Creative Commons License 2.0. Source: https://www.flickr.com/photos/derekskey/5249593792/in/set-72157625570278728

p. 242: Photo used courtesy of the Library of Congress

p. 286: Painting by Adriaen Coorte, 1697; photo from Wikimedia, used under Creative Commons License 2.0. Source: http://commons.wikimedia.org/wiki/File:Adriaen_Corte_-_Still_Life_with_Asparagus.jpg

A NOTE ABOUT THE AUTHOR

Jane Hirshfield is the author of eight books of poetry, including *The Beauty*; *Come, Thief*; *After*; and *Given Sugar, Given Salt*. She has edited and cotranslated four books presenting the work of poets from the past and is the author of two major collections of essays, *Nine Gates: Entering the Mind of Poetry* and *Ten Windows: How Great Poems Transform the World*. Her books have been finalists for the National Book Critics Circle Award and England's T. S. Eliot Prize; they have been named best books of the year by *The Washington Post*, *San Francisco Chronicle*, Amazon, and *Financial Times*; and they have won the California Book Award, the Poetry Center Book Award, and the Donald Hall–Jane Kenyon Prize in American Poetry. Hirshfield has received fellowships from the Guggenheim and Rockefeller foundations, the National Endowment for the Arts, and the Academy of American Poets. Her poems appear in *The New Yorker*, *The Atlantic*, *The Times Literary Supplement*, *Poetry*, *The New Republic*, and seven editions of *The Best American Poetry*. A resident of Northern California since 1974, she is a current chancellor of the Academy of American Poets.

A NOTE ON THE TYPE

The text of this book was set in Requiem, a typeface designed by Jonathan Hoefler (born 1970) and released in the late 1990s by the Hoefler Type Foundry. It was derived from a set of inscriptional capitals appearing in Ludovico Vicentino degli Arrighi's 1523 writing manual, *Il Modo di Temperare le Penne*. A master scribe, Arrighi is remembered as an exemplar of the chancery italic, a style revived in Requiem Italic.

Composed by North Market Street Graphics, Lancaster, Pennsylvania

Printed and bound by Berryville Graphics, Berryville, Virginia

Designed by Iris Weinstein